T A N N I N G
TECHNOLOGY CORPORATION

Tanning Technology is setting the new standard for systems integration worldwide. Moving organisations' business strategies in the Internet age from concept to reality, Tanning conquers large, complex, integration challenges that incorporate online transaction processing, very large databases and highly distributed computing. Tanning architects, builds and deploys the backbone of company information technology infrastructures to support collaborative, rapid-growth and evolving business models. Through the unique net Marketplace Integration™ Framework and Service Level Assurance™ Methodology, Tanning Consultants are experienced providers of business solutions in the areas of customer channel integration, financial trading and asset management, custom IT solutions and net marketplace implementation and integration. More information on Tanning can be found at www.tanning.com.

GEOFF **WEBB**

THE **M**-BO*M*B

Riding the
Multi-channel Whirlwind

CAPSTONE

First published 2001 by
Capstone Publishing, Inc.
40 Commerce Park
Milford
CT 06460
USA
Contact: info@capstonepub.com

Capstone Publishing Limited
8 Newtec Place
Oxford OX4 1RE
United Kingdom
http://www.capstone.co.uk

CIP catalogue records for this book are available from the British Library and the US Library of Congress

ISBN 1-84112-139-8

Typeset in 11/14 pt Caslon No. 224 by
Sparks Computer Solutions Ltd, Oxford, UK
http://www.sparks.co.uk
Printed and bound by
TJ International Ltd, Padstow, Cornwall

This book is printed on acid-free paper

Substantial discounts on bulk quantities of Capstone books are available to corporations, professional associations and other organizations. If you are in the USA or Canada, phone the LPC Group, Special Sales Department for details on (1-800-626-4330) or fax (1-800-334-3892). Everywhere else, phone Capstone Publishing on (+44-1865-798623) or fax (+44-1865-240941).

"The M-Bomb"

- The early e-commerce bubbles have already started to burst and are now giving way to highly credible and profitable multi-channel services which meet real customer needs and make money.
- The arrival of this new generation of convenient and efficient services from both established and new players is shining a torch in the eyes of traditional success stories. Many of the best brands in the world are hopelessly ill-equipped for this challenge.
- Both old-economy and dotcom businesses are facing the m-bomb – the multi-channel challenge which forces every business to engineer how products can be delivered efficiently at home as well as in the high street, online as well as through old-world sales forces or enticing shopping centers. Fail to solve this and your costs explode – and your competitiveness collapses.
- This book is a comprehensive guide for both the new- and the old-economy businesses which will help them to thrive and to survive the m-bomb. Very few businesses have been able to successfully manage clicks, bricks and other tricks in a way which is smooth and profitable. Brand is still king – but only 20% of the brands we know, large and small, will survive under their current leadership in the next five years – as the winners learn to serve customers in any way which they individually choose – face-to-face, Internet, phone, personalized services …
- The Internet on its own is a damp squib. This is an integration thing. A pick 'n' mix, plug 'n' play, best of both worlds thing.

Contents

Contents

Foreword

I found myself plummeting. My left side was hitting what felt like concrete and my right side was bouncing off something soft and uneven. After what seemed like an age I hit the bottom, lurching to a stop as my feet embedded themselves into some sort of rancid mush.

I looked up, and realized with a sense of relief that I could still see the African sky, with the stars winking down at me through the dark circle above my head. The pain then started to come in waves, complemented by the exquisite realization that I was wearing the "smart casual" trousers that I was expecting to wear the following day for my keynote speech to the breweries conference. I couldn't actually see the muddy designs and tears on the trousers, but for some bizarre reason the threat of public embarrassment worried me much more than my hand, which was sending out distress signals like a gale-struck trawler. An indescribable smell made me look down into the inky blackness. I wanted to see if I could make out the bloated corpse of a dead goat or perhaps a baboon who had come off worst in a territorial dispute. There are times though when action is more important than understanding.

I crawled up out of the hole using a lot of elbows and knees and stood shakily on the grass. It was good to be alive. The clean mountain air flushed through my airways like a tonic, almost sensually. I carefully picked my way back to the hotel – 50 yards of the nervous "Santa Claus" walk (which you use when you have just put the children's presents down by the bed) and then a spell of moonwalking as I triumphantly reached the floodlit area.

The woman behind the counter looked up at me with mild disgust as I burst into the lobby, earth colors and the unspeakable decorating my body. I was making a mess of her nice hotel and in danger of frightening some of the sophisticated American guests who were staying. I told her my story in my typically apologetic English way, and suggested that some lighting and barriers might be prudent. Nothing doing. She made it clear with her thinly veneered look of concern that it was my fault. She was careful not to patronize me too obviously, but she did point out that guests don't get swimming pools without someone digging holes for pumps and things. Lights would be installed quite soon, so nothing really to worry about was there sir?

Oh well.

In fact I was relatively lucky, as I found out the next morning. I could easily have fallen in the pool itself. This lay a few yards further on, its empty concrete mouth yawning quietly in the morning sun. If I had taken a slightly different path, I would have broken both legs and possibly something more serious.

The laundry was of course shut for the night. Were Mandela himself staying, there would have been no possibility of waking Doris, who was the only one who could operate heavy equipment such as the steam pump and the automated sheep dip. I soon tired of my pathetic efforts to advance the situation and slunk off to my room. I could have used a cuddle, but my wife was five thousand miles away, and I didn't fancy the old lady who was fiddling with her Hoover attachments by the garbage area.

I was soon back on track again when I reached my room. I managed some judicious "trouser juggling," which I won't go into here, and had an enjoyable few hours in the elegant bathroom, scraping mud off my handstitched Italian shoes and out of my ears and hair.

As often happens in these bittersweet situations, I survived the conference the next morning in surprisingly good shape and found the company of the brewers and their strategic reconnaissance to be thoroughly enjoyable. Lots of buzz, gently choreographed excitement and the odd Tom Cruise lookalike added to the hands-on, "mission impossible" style of theatre. Another day, another mood, another world. The helicopter ride back up through the Drakensburg escarpment to Johannesburg airport was a real Belgian-chocolate finish to a most remarkable 24 hours.

The strange experience of finding an unlit and undefended man-trap that night, which diverted me and almost wrecked my plans, serves as a suitable introduction to the content of this book. I find that for the large and ambitious businesses that I work with around the world the "one true path" is getting much harder to find and the potholes are getting deeper. Exploration and recovery periods are becoming ever shorter and are requiring increasingly unfamiliar skills (and emotions). The forces unleashed by the Internet and the explosion of new ways of reaching customers have allowed radically new and effective business models to come in out of nowhere. The early phase of activity linked to the Internet and new marketplaces were mostly puff and wind, but what is starting now is both real and fundamental. It will effectively kill off over half of today's big-league brands and players.

The benchmark for marketing innovation and organizational efficiency has shifted faster in the last two years than at any time in history. The froth surrounding the young kids who led the first cavalry charge with their saddlebags full of easy VC money is now subsiding, and the real war is beginning. These are the multi-channel wars – where the most powerful businesses and brands will compete to master the complex skills of servicing customers in a range of new and more convenient ways, without compromising their traditional operations which keep today's profit engines turning. This is the m-bomb.

The m-bomb represents the challenge which faces all businesses to build a set of convenient and efficient multi-channel operations and routes to market which bridge the old and the new worlds (Monday Mary will browse on the high street, Tuesday she will pop in online and buy some things she knows she needs, Wednesday she will receive her usual bulk home service using her preferred delivery method). At work, a similar blend of face-to-face, phone, online and direct and indirect channels will play together efficiently to help her business run smoothly. It is a huge test for both old and new-economy businesses, because all businesses have to learn how to take success and dominance in one channel through to the full range of channels that customers will demand. Today's best pioneers are now achieving these feats without adding significant costs. You have to restructure your operations quickly, or new upstarts and agile competitors will gradually siphon off many of your best customers by offering them services that you can't – convenience, choices, order here, deliver there, serve me in special ways. The Internet is there in these new models, but is working more behind the scenes than in the more trivial "in your face" ways.

The m-bomb is causing the routes to customers' hearts and wallets to explode around us. Most businesses understand well the role of the high street and traditional customer advertising and mass retailing – but we now can add communication demands for home PCs, smart phones, digital TV and a raft of new home delivery and fulfillment services which offer magical new product opportunities and brand relationships. Charting your way through the myths and realities of how the Internet and new service models will change our businesses is the stuff of life now for most executives. Or at least it is for those who are alert to the barometer which is starting to fall sharply.

Some of the change in the markets, and the way that the competitive metabolism is lifting rapidly, is not just surprising but is really shocking to many CEOs. I speak to many business leaders during my travels, who see the bets that other businesses are placing and feel that their own choices for action are becoming bewildering. So many competing demands for resources. So many potential new entrants and competitive moves. Pressure to place bets on how fast customers will move to the new online channels and how the role of high streets and direct-sales operations will change. So many academic business models to consider, dripping optimistically from the intellectual section of every bookstore.

How the needs of typical families and bigger spenders are diversifying is the real key to where much of the future lies. For many reasons the evolution of the economics of supply and service and of consumer buying behaviors has become my passion, my quest for the source of the Nile, my daytime companion as I and my colleagues work on a confusing array of e-commerce and multi-channel implementations around the world.

This book is designed to entertain as much as my modest writing skills will allow. More importantly, it aims to offer practical help to business people who need to better understand how to tackle these changes in the way that business is done within the next three years. It is founded upon my frenetically developed experience of driving change and service innovation across international consumer goods, entertainment, financial services, everyday retail and a raft of other weird and wonderful sectors. We have had to learn the hard way how to weave the old-economy skills of product innovation and retailing together with the hard recent lessons of multi-channel Internet innovation. I have been hugely impressed and personally challenged by a broad and breathless participation in these last five dog-years of e-services and multi-channel pioneering across many sectors. I say dog-years, because every team I have been thrown together with has been working like a dog and has been driving change at at least seven times the pace that your priest or mother would recommend. We have together accumulated hundreds of man-years of operational e-business and traditional invention across five continents, on top of the hundreds of multi-channel innovations which we have observed and analyzed to improve our understanding of this sea-change in the markets.

In one sector or another, I can now personally admit to a range of mistakes and salutary lessons in every aspect of reinventing product development, procurement, supply-chain and customer service, spanning the office to the high street to the home. In the early days of the m-clouds gathering we used to make the promise that we would develop or transform your operations and services and get you in the market in six months or your money back – so it is lucky that we still have the shirts on our backs.

The book is also designed to draw on experience going back much further, in order to help those who are developing new products, services and profit streams to avoid that plummeting feeling, the blood-loss, the tarnished image and the messy recovery that I see everywhere in many successful businesses which used to act with such confidence and certainty (and that I felt in more tangible form a year ago when I fell down the hole in the Drakensburg mountains). The business and personal utilities which are growing on the Internet, the strange new alliances and buying clubs, the opportunities to reshape your customer connection and the era of "customer intimate operations" is changing their landscape and the important skillsets that all businesses require. We are all seeing the giants of yesterday stumble, and yet many of them are perfectly placed to exploit their great brands and scale so that they can dance to these new tunes.

Traditional businesses are really much better equipped to manage the m-world than any new entrant – they just don't know how to harness their powerful business development and functional skills so that they can offer customers a choice of ways to order and a choice of ways to receive a more rounded and convenient set of services. Many of the answers are not hard to find – but they are usually obscured by the siren voices of irrelevant technologies or implausible grand schemes which lack focus. Sometimes the main problem is just that the First World War generals are sitting ten miles behind the lines and can't see the new trenches.

A personal discovery of the multi-channel game

So why do I worry so much about the m-bomb, stumbling giants and the more substantial type of "feet on the ground" start-ups that I also get emotionally involved in?

My parents came from the rougher end of Salford in the North of England and were considered posh at their local schools because they wore shoes. Their approach to community and the powerful support network that they have fostered over the years has been very effective for them. Their values and approach to collective effort and community support have influenced me more than I usually will admit. Traces of this background and the sense of many unfamiliar hills to be climbed have led me, from my early years in business, to be ambitious and keen to find some extra pace for the team that I am part of. That has usually translated into probing and experimenting with almost every aspect of how we did things, whilst also learning to cope with the smaller successes and failures of delivering the numbers along the way.

I loved my 15 years at the start of my working life at Unilever (a $50bn consumer-goods conglomerate operating in 75 countries). I loved the fact that they let me work as a house-trained revolutionary while I stumbled up the cargo net. I was allowed to experiment and evolve my ideas in most of the corners of their operations, ultimately as an integral part of every line role and command function I held. I still keep my shares in Unilever today because I believe in the power of individual invention which is woven into the fabric of the business, although like many great businesses you only realize how open the culture is when you have left.

Unilever has been a multi-channel business of sorts for many years, with a core set of products and services able to be driven through direct channels to bakeries or hospitals and also indirect retail channels such as OK Bazaars, K-Mart and Carrefour. The new options of online consumer at home, consumer on the phone and consumer in the partner's store is not such a great stretch from what we learnt to plug and play together across the product divisions and territories. It just seems more uncertain and frightening now because the bets are much greater. The consumers are starting to move the goalposts and diverge their requirements at a pace we have never seen before.

I have since, in a very short time, had the good fortune to develop my nose for driving customer-led change with a large number of successful and aggressive blue-chip businesses. To augment this experience, much of which forms the basis of the book, I have also touched over five hundred smaller businesses (in one way or another). By accident rather than design, I tend to get dragged into projects which involve major change in products, channels and service but with relatively little time or money. The impatience and urgency of business leaders is visibly growing, in line with their increasing distaste for large consultancy projects or plodding internal assessments which deliver recycled packs of acetates and little action.

It is particularly worrying that the bigger the company the more money is locked away in feeding the traditional and well-understood operations, rather than growing new distribution and service foundations and root systems. For this reason (and perhaps a form of new-economy snow-blindness), the defense mechanisms for the multi-channel bomb that is now descending rapidly are not being deployed at all in some of the larger businesses. In very large businesses the purse strings can be guarded by cumbersome committee processes or by the least imaginative or the most cautious in the business. In the years of stable customer needs this is a true blessing. At times like this, when the customer-facing fault-lines need to be reconstructed, it can be a pillow gently applied to the face. On the plus side though, I have also recently witnessed a handful of truly great innovation and distribution strategies, founded on careful but smart iteration of "what we are already doing" – a feat of multi-channel engineering which dovetails the needs of different types of customer and which sparks new life in the existing business in many dramatic ways.

The book is therefore also my personal way of bottling and fermenting my years of conspiring to change and develop Unilever from the inside as I shinned up the greasy pole, as well as with Barclays (Retail Financial Services where customer channels have been detonated by phone banking and the Internet) and then countless other bluechips who I now touch as they drive aggressive change programs and create new profit streams. The mistakes that I have been involved with and contributed to would also make entertaining reading, but I was worried that it wouldn't sell as well! (I will make those the sequel.)

From being involved in so many conceptions and births now, in such a short time, I have automatically absorbed and distilled the simple touchstones that are fundamental to weaving wonderfully divergent consumer needs into multi-channel supply chains and enduring relationships which will make money. We can all now see the fluffier or flatulent dotcoms failing as they lack the volumes and the brand heritage of the established mass-market offers. We also see the plodding big boys wasting buckets of cash and stalling in the market, because they cannot see how to weave powerful and profitable new online propositions alongside their traditional profit streams. This is now a world where a strong predatory brand (like Walmart, Nike or Chase) can use smartly designed services and products made by good partners to come in and build a franchise for a profitable group of consumers in just two years.

The new rules of the m-world are emerging clearly. If you are an established global player then you already have the brand and many vital skills and assets. It is really inexcusable for you not to reshape your organization and forge the alliances you will need to be one of those evergreen brands who will thrive in the new market – one of the 20% or so of today's brands that will rule the earth after the dust from the m-bomb has settled.

For me, these touchstones and the new business approaches which fill the next chapters are the very stuff of life. This is not just about business survival in your current niche, it is far more important than that. The tectonic plates are moving rapidly and the consumers and service economics are forming much richer patterns than they were ever able to do in the past. An organization's response cannot be instinctively functional or traditional – that won't do it any more. As new currents form and move faster in the sea, so the successful predators must observe and learn from each other and learn to hunt together. Each learning cycle is now only six to nine months long. Very few companies have really had to react to this before. Services which can reach customers any way that they want will require businesses to partner with compatible companies; those that can offer different ways to service customers on the move and at home, provide both online and traditional services for billing/procurement/sales/marketing, introduce the right adjacent products and services to broaden the offer and deliver a small number of other capabilities which enable all the parties to reach sufficient numbers of profitable customers.

The remainder of the book is my way of describing the music and the practical moves, which the winners will need to perform the dances in these more turbulent waters. The consumer of course is the funny looking guy, with the flippers and goggles which come in six hundred different speeds and colors.

Introduction

Let's face it – the Internet hasn't yet touched the vast majority of households or the way that we live our lives. The first fluffy years have certainly seen lots of useful bits and pieces happening in personal communication, travel and banking. Unfortunately most of the puff and wind has come from established brands developing pathetic Websites, while dotcoms screamed loudly and expensively in the slot next to Ally McBeal, like a little rich kid who no one recognizes or wants to hear.

The shock wave of the Internet hasn't come close to hitting yet – whatever the hype says. So is the Internet really just a fashion statement, a side show, an e-mail and sex thing?

Wrong question! It has never been about the Internet. The Internet on its own is a damp squib. The traditional business isn't dead and brand is a bigger king than ever before. This is an integration thing. A pick 'n' mix, plug 'n' play, best of both worlds thing.

The new competitive battle is for the major brands to extend what they do. They must reorganize themselves to touch existing and new customers in both traditional channels and online channels, at high levels of efficiency. They must create the business model to fold partner skills and products in with their own, to offer a steady stream of services and product innovation across these different channels. Different types of customer able to get precisely what they want, how they want.

This transformation is hard to achieve. Most businesses around the world are either hypnotized by the siren voices of the pure Internet options or are in denial and placing bets on the status quo. Many dotcoms are in even greater trouble because they don't even have the established brand, let alone the mix of traditional channels and skills to anchor their offer.

This fundamental challenge is the m-bomb, and it will push into new ownership or just kill off up to 80% of today's successful brands over the next five years. This is because the costs of managing efficient multi-channel supply chains, marketing, communications and customer services will go ballistic if you just tinker with how you currently do things. Some smart investment and vision is required to communicate across the old and new media and to touch and service customers in ways that they will respond to. The businesses which can organize themselves quickly to master the multi-channel game will do hugely well, as they sweep up the diamonds in the debris from those operations which can't evolve their brands and services fast enough.

In Part 1 we will explore why the m-bomb is ticking and distil the evidence we see around us in the markets, of who is losing the plot and who is getting there. We look at some of the hills to climb as well as some reasons to smile a little.

In Part 2 we look at how to create the strategy, organization and business agenda for the next five years. By distilling the lessons from 1000 company years of real multi-channel innovation we will detail the practical changes, business approaches and actions that you will need to take in your business. Every insight has a market anecdote and a practical example or two. If you are anxious to go straight to the meat of what you must do (and go back to why you must do it later), then jump straight to page 35 now.

In Part 3 we look at how to implement the changes and how to create the environment and culture which will accept and accelerate the new customer offers and revenue streams. We cover the ways that you must build and experiment, as well as the ways to kick the "thought police" out of the way.

In Part 4 we summarize the immediate steps the winning businesses will need to take and look forward to some more mini-bombs and future trends to track and watch out for.

Tick, tick, tick, tick …

Part 1

Hearing the M-Bomb Ticking

Chapter 1

Life Beyond the

Internet Clouds

There are some things that we can be certain about, which businesses need to respond to as they move into the practical phase of building multi-channel businesses:

- Managers in traditional businesses with great ideas find it much, much harder to get funding than fashionable joint ventures which span many businesses (e.g. the new buying clubs like Transora which raised over $200m in a few months). This is despite the fact that traditional businesses have cheaper access to funds. Companies like Unilever have a triple A credit rating – so they can borrow more cheaply than most banks and could use their cash to retain all the equity, if they so chose. I recently was able to raise a sum of money in just two days from a venture capitalist that would have taken me nine months of serious lobbying, planning and justification in any normal large business.

  I am constantly being approached by smart people in blue chips who are dying from frustration because of this problem. They usually feel that they must leave if they want to be able to pursue their dreams without being hamstrung. (All that the best and most experienced ones want to hear is "have $500k my boy – go and follow your instincts – you can have 2% of the equity also!") Having lost some of the sharpest people, who could bridge the old and the new worlds with great personal knowledge and experience, the company will often then pay a fortune to consultants for similar advice.

- Most large businesses are to entrepreneurial partnering, what mix-amatosis is to rabbits. True partnering is not about thrashing out a half-decent product spec and then paying in 30 days (using online self-billing to reduce admin costs for both sides). In the multi-channel, post-modernist Internet world, partnering is about trusting each other to co-design and transform the product development cycle and to outsource huge chunks of the fulfillment or buying process. Partnering is about combining complementary product and service skills from a number of different specialist businesses, to take away a whole need or problem area for your customers. This is a part of what Hewlett-Packard call Chapter 2 of the Internet – creating step-changes in time to market and customer convenience, working capital, operational efficiency/response etc. New configurations of service businesses and "applications on tap" can transform the overheads you need to carry within the business. Look at what guys like Merita (a Swedish bank), Gall & Gall (a Dutch wine retailer, www.gall.nl), Tesco (UK retailer), Chase or BT (telecoms) are doing in building compelling new multi-channel offers, using powerful partners in specialist areas to augment their internal skills.
- You can typically generate a lot more shareholder value by developing a creative multi-channel proposition than by selling another million tubs of yogurt. It may be unfair in your mind – but life's a bitch. Procter and Gamble are starting to understand this. Their "Reflect" service for personalized cosmetics is exactly what an indirect brand player needs to do to make new money, while avoiding arguments with their existing channel partners like Walmart. This new brand offers tailored products direct to the consumer – so they learn about them, engage with them intimately (a novelty for an indirect manufacturer) and make money from a product that doesn't compete head on with the existing retail channel. If it continues to grow, it becomes a high-value new-economy asset on the balance sheet. Don't just sell more wine and beer – make it easy for them to stock all their weekend and party needs from you. Get the delivery and home replenishment sorted at zero cost while you are about it. Whilst you are doing this, keep selling the wine and beer on the high street as well.

- How much is your product really viewed as unique and must-have? Brand and product loyalty is becoming significantly overstated in most businesses. As you look across most consumer and business-to-business sectors, the existing service is relatively poor value in terms of what is now possible. Most customers are loyal partly because of inertia. A wonderbrand that offered a similar product or service in a more convenient or personalized way would probably capture more than a quarter of the market, if nothing else changed. If Nokia, GE or Microsoft were to badge a television, which was remarkably easy to buy online or from home and was reviewed as a best buy in consumer magazines, then how many consumers would bother to click through two more pages or hunt for a store to find a brand like Panasonic? This may sound cynical but we have found that research and recent experience bears it out. Are you really delighted with your bank, your travel agent, your career adviser, your builder/plumber/electrician, your newspaper, your raw materials supplier, and your healthcare service? *Write down on a piece of paper the six brands or services you would always stay loyal to even if you had to work hard to find them. Think then how your customers would categorize your business.*

- Brand is still king – but only a small number of the major brands that we know and love today will be able to secure "share of voice" in the multi-channel world and survive independently in the next five years. Many businesses who are the stewards of the world's best brands are currently ill equipped to handle this and are relatively rudderless. They know about those old and easy tactics to target customers, where you booked the advertising slot next to Frasier, but they have no mental context at all for deciding how to communicate the brand in the multi-channel world, which includes personalized services and a range of ways of talking to customers via the Internet. The Guinnesses and the Gaps of this world seem to get it – but it seems that organizations like Cartier and Nestlé are dazzled in the headlights.

- Companies need to acquire some important new competencies very fast, and shed some others which no longer make a difference. The key skills of the next three years include the way you drive customer relationships (as you really touch the customer each week, rather than just the dry database stuff), integrated marketing (brand contacts across in-store, TV, online, phone…), product innovation and service integration (managing development partners and end-to-end delivery/performance).

- For many reasons you can see the aggressive traditional players and the really dangerous start-ups focusing ruthlessly on acquiring these skills and then buying in almost everything else. The bulk of established businesses find it hard to place priority and direct resources against these competencies, which are usually what differentiates you in the market. *For these businesses most resources go into tickling yesterday's familiar activities like manufacturing, which customers only really see if they go wrong. These are competencies which you can now buy in, very cost effectively, from a range of specialist vertical businesses which have emerged.* Many senior managers are traditional marketeers or highly promoted accountants or factory managers – they won't feel comfortable about placing big bets on these new competency areas and it is also hard to diminish the importance of your own heartland and those of your colleagues. The resourcing actions rarely get to match the well intentioned acetates of the international strategy they have bought in.

- Customers are less loyal to niche or standalone products than we ever realized. If they are offered bundled services which take their whole problem away, from someone they trust, customers immediately tend to trust the quality of all the components. One simple example is CarPoint. When you buy a car from them you get offered insurance, breakdown services and many other added value services. Consumer research tells us that apparently most Americans would rather have root canal surgery than talk to a car salesman – so using an online or direct-service integrator who can broker in lots of allied services is just really convenient. Time is precious these days.

- Similarly I may want a holiday in Mexico – I want to know about the best place to see (and I don't want to spend $20 on a Michelin guide which includes lots of rambling prose about agriculture and the history of the ruling classes in small towns that I will never visit). I also want holiday cover, flights, hotels, car hire … it's just easier than shopping around separately and talking to people I don't really feel that loyal to. Is it any wonder that getthere.com are projected to do well if they continue to tie into traditional channels intelligently, whilst most sites from respected travel brands are fairly pathetic and their shares are down. It was great to see Amex buying GetThere to kick-start their realignment and to see that the new club of major airlines (BA, Air France, Lufthansa etc.) are using GetThere's services to deliver their new online travel agencies. These should do very well if they can learn to work together. The old and the new working together.

- Why can't someone you trust deliver all your everyday grocery products, DIY bits and pieces, videos, wine and newspapers to your house at no charge each week? But you get the point. If I don't specify Hershey Chocolate or I just say "your best house wine" my brand purchase decision is made or influenced by the service broker. You'd better be there with these new propositions or your volume will drop by that crucial 15% and your P&L collapses in a heap. Why aren't more branded-goods players occupying the blindingly obvious brokering positions, or developing the wider customer propositions? Why are so few traditional financial-services brokers driving in new consumer supermarket services? Is it dark in here or am I just wearing sunglasses?

- Up to 50% of senior management in more traditional businesses may need to move on very, very quickly – they will try hard to get a feel for the multi-channel world but they just won't get it. Compromise in this area is death. The speed of decision making and action is everything in this new market place. *If in doubt I would suggest that a business leader who wants to develop the profit model should re-deploy the successful executive who doesn't see the need for applied creativity to a close competitor.*

Taken together these forces already represent quite a leadership challenge for those at the helm.

To further focus the mind for the strategies, investments and defenses needed to profit from the m-bomb, I wanted to draw out some other facts and issues which influence life beyond the Internet clouds.

When taken together they convince the more thoughtful people I speak with that we are in the midst of the equivalent of a medieval flu epidemic – killing off the weak and testing the mettle of absolutely everyone:

1 Older players are coming off the bench to join this new game. The spotty youths of the first Internet wave are making way for the experienced Titans. Boo.com was bound to fail in Europe due to a yawning lack of management experience from its founders, but watch out for the new wave of experienced players. Forget whether the Internet has lit the fire or whether it has also been fanned by the globalization of media, supply chains, customer needs or capitalism. Everywhere you look we see old mates with 20 years experience leaving for 3% of a new financial services play from an established brand.

2 Remember how you once said in the bar that if you could take the best forty operators, creatives and leaders from your current multinational (the sharpest 40 from the 20,000 top managers), you could redesign the whole thing, cut out the ludicrous committee processes and make ten times as much money. Well, they are doing it now, using the new economy as an excuse. You must have thought about it yourself – it beats flogging your guts out in the engine room for another 15 years (or twiddling your thumbs in early retirement).

3 New businesses and mixed-economy spin-offs are emerging which can serve global markets with a few hundred permanent staff. These are not Mickey-Mouse operations and they change the benchmark for agility, employee efficiency, organizational metabolism and the very meaning of partnering.

4 Even if you can't reinvent your internal operations quickly, can you at least learn to form close partnerships as easily as Ford – who have linked with UPS to handle the logistics of car delivery. I find a car manufacturer giving its life-threatening logistics problems to a logistics player both obvious and surprising at the same time (that they had the courage to partner in this way – and saved so much money doing it).

5 Consumers and customers are getting used to the sort of personalization that they can get from Kickers, Reflect or Amazon. Some of the more unreasonable ones are now expecting the same intimacy in the other services they use. If you are geared up properly it is

cheap and easy to offer customers personalized services and product offers and it tells you a lot about your customers. If you are not geared up for it in advance, it can flatten your margins overnight (personalized products and services are expensive to graft onto an inflexible single-channel business).

6 They used to say that half of your television advertising was wasted, but you did not know which half. You ain't seen nothing yet with the explosion of TV and online channels. To try to add some science in the new channels, some companies believe that cookies (electronic tags which sites can plant on you) are a great online mechanism to track every site or service a consumer visits and to recognize them when they come back. A dangerous game. You risk freaking out half your customers and invading their privacy. Perhaps you should just give them the right offers and level of intimacy in a less invasive way.

7 The Internet has now arrived in Mogadishu. Only three African countries don't have an ISP now. So as long as you don't get posted to the Congo or Eritrea you can reach your favorite services from almost anywhere in the world. Adult Internet penetration in Washington and Stockholm is now over 50%. It is clear that the Internet is here forever and it will contribute to subtle changes to the way many of your customers hear about your products, buy them and complain (to everyone) about them. No one can afford to go into denial. A bunch of pathetic dotcoms failing is irrelevant.

8 As we mentioned earlier, the easiest path to generating shareholder value does not lie in selling a million more toothpaste dispensers. Sad – because your business may be very comfortable in knowing how to do that – but true. Some new-economy and Internet bubbles will continue to burst as the future gets reinvented, but not the bubble machine that enables a powerful range of new propositions every month – sector by sector. As customer needs and expectations change, bit by bit, there will be lots of little angles to aim for which can generate huge amounts of shareholder value. If you don't aim high and take a few risks at the margins you will never "double shareholder value in three years" – as most businesses seem to have committed to do.

9 The years of one market subsidizing another are almost over. Companies like British Airways and Ford have spent years making more

money for the same product in some markets than others. The UK is famous for having much higher prices for the same cars and electrical products than other countries in Europe or in the US. The Internet means that companies will be hit by transparency of pricing and will need to be cost-competitive regionally and globally or they will die – and deservedly so. Artificial subsidies which block genuine competition are a crutch, and ultimately they do not serve the invalid well.

I like the Big Mac index, which reveals whether currencies are correctly valued and whether beef, ketchup and commercial property prices are sensibly aligned in the local country. If a Big-Mac is more expensive in your country than in Dayton, Ohio then that tells you a lot about your personal cost of living and your relative national competitiveness (or efficiency). If your company's products cost more in Germany than in Spain then you have more fundamental reasons to worry – your P&L may be built on sand which will give way as international transparency cuts in.

10 Please don't judge the new channels and the e-business services by what you see out there today. The elephants have been breeding quietly behind the barns and the offspring are ready to rampage in your vegetable patch over the next year or two. *What you see now is a shadow of what will be.*

So these facts and forces give some strong indications for later chapters of where your business strategy should go and what changes are now becoming urgent. In most sectors you need to address this seriously right now.

Maarten Dorhout-Mees of Royal Ahold (Group Director of Strategy) summarizes how some of the largest and the best traditional businesses in the world are gradually reinventing themselves to secure their share of the future:

> "e-commerce and a range of service choices will very soon be 'business as usual' for consumers in retail and an integral part of the offer. Today's market leaders will lose out in a big way if they are not prepared to service their customers properly in this multi-channel world."

Your role as the forward-looking skeptic

To make sure that we don't leap from the hot plate into the waste disposal I believe that any chief executive worth their salt will still ask some very basic questions.

- *How can I make money from this within three to five years?* Is it likely to be a better prospect for making or saving money than the other handful of great ideas that my executives are screaming for? The existence of m-opportunities do not mean that all other bets are off.
- *Does a broader or more accessible service meet a real need for customers who we are good at serving?* If not, why should we be taking this forward? (It may be a good idea – but not one for us.) Said more simply, this is trying to ask whether giving customers one-touch access to your existing services at home via PC, TV or smart-phone wouldn't be better than moving into soft furnishings. In impulse sectors for example, the customer will consume a lot more product if it is easy to get at. The costs of logistics and online ordering for the last twenty miles is now down to the price point when you can cost-effectively replenish beer kegs at home – so you can now think whether customers will respond positively if you add a beer tap to the hot and cold taps in the kitchen. I know that this simple facility would make me drink like a fish. I would rather my local brewery offered me this service than an online choice of branded sweatshirts and boozy holidays in Munich.
- *If I support the ambitious changes, how will we ensure that we can implement them robustly as an integral part of our business?* Has the proposal been shaped to grasp the opportunity in the best way, with sensible initial outlay, early checkpoints etc. Quick and innovative does not equal dirty. There is no excuse for poor operational delivery or lack of commercial plans and milestones, as many breathless start-ups have realized – the Website is a tiny part of getting the end-to-end fulfillment and execution service right.

A leader who blindly bets the whole business on a half-baked Internet gamble or on rapid global expansion is serving no-one. In the different sections of this book we try to address how established businesses should embark on colonizing the future and surviving the m-bomb, without forgetting their company's knitting and what they are good at – and what customers value. Executive teams must move forward in the knowledge that most of the common-sense rules still apply to creating customer-centric operations and lower-cost businesses. They just need to be applied within a different framework and they require some different competencies to be acquired very quickly.

To learn to fly you don't just strap a bunch of dead birds to your arms – you must analyze the challenge intelligently and construct a plan to create a much lighter superstructure and approach to how you do things.

Most of the big brands and multinationals are still in the process of strapping dead birds to their arms as they develop their first knee-jerk e-services operations. As part of the day job, my colleagues and I maintain a comprehensive library of the best and worst Internet and multi-channel services that are currently out there in each sector, and we see the shambles caused by the unimaginative and the "act of faith" merchants all the time. I talk more about what we find there in Part 2.

It is quite surprising to see where both the practical and more radical consumer innovation is coming from at the moment. A handful of established businesses are really on the ball, but a huge number of highly credible businesses are doing things that are truly pathetic – an embarrassment to themselves and a signal to customers, desperate for more efficient services, that they are likely to be clueless for the foreseeable future. I will describe later how we categorize and evaluate the new channels, propositions and services that businesses are building. Using our measures of business common sense and genuine usefulness to customers it seems that 90% of established businesses are out to lunch. It is really better to do nothing at all than to put your brand out there in a state of undress, and yet a high proportion of the *Fortune* 500 have misinterpreted the opportunities and the customer needs and are just playing with home-shopping services or throwing out vacuous Websites which offer nothing of any value.

The really good news is that the market is there for the taking for those who can walk and chew gum in this complicated but exciting world. There are some new rules for the multi-channel game, and if you can draw from the experience of the pioneers and build upon your traditional skills and values which are still of immense value then great things lie in front of you.

In the chapters that follow we will lay out how the new rules of the game will work alongside the old ones, and distil the experience that we have developed from across the different business sectors (from getting it wrong sometimes as well as the hard-won successes). We will now go into more detail on the challenges in the next section – which will hopefully help you to release the trapped wind and prepare the body corporate for the m-bomb and the organizational Viagra that you will need to take.

Chapter 2 goes a little deeper into the background for change, so if you are impatient I would jump straight to Part 2.

Chapter 2

Reasons to Smile
and then Panic (a Little)

The early days of the Internet really have been pretty disappointing. The technologies have only seriously affected the way in which companies have operated in information-based sectors and the way in which some of the smarter companies have taken a few billion out of their basic business transactions in areas like purchasing. In books, share dealing, music and travel, the Web has indeed created some genuine seismic shifts in the way that services are delivered in the lead markets. When looked at soberly though, the impact on the guy in the street has been minimal and the vast majority of profit generated by the *Fortune* 500 companies and the GDP of the G7 countries still comes from traditional businesses, selling products in traditional ways. The shock wave of the Internet is still rippling out there on the distant horizon for most of us.

What has hit is that companies, large and small, have started to spend money on cobbling together new and often asinine online services. We call them "the chairman's son" sites, where it looks like a well-connected kid has knocked up something quickly to get on the Web. Many companies have done this without knowing how to link their embarrassing and tawdry Websites to their existing retail or manufacturing operations and their current customer relationships. They know they are building these exploratory "bits and pieces" in a way which is adding cost for little tangible gain – but they feel that they should be doing something.

Conversely the first wave of dotcoms have developed interesting new online propositions, but they usually have no real idea how to migrate large numbers of "typical" consumers to use their services.

Businesses like Letsbuyit, Lastminute and Webvan will always struggle to reach the mass market until they can provide deeper anchors and signposts in the physical world. Most consumers aren't quite ready to shift a lot of their buying behavior to pure online services. Their personal bloodbaths will continue until they learn to reinforce their brands and services in traditional channels.

Most businesses realize they must learn to change or die. However, only a handful of companies have worked out how to efficiently bridge the old and the new and are now playing the multi-channel game in a way which will deliver profitable volume. To be successful, a consumer business must be able to reach anyone from my mother, who happens to be very traditional, to my "bit of both" brother, to my pointy-headed son, without compromising efficiency and operating margins. This neither sounds easy, nor is easy. A small number of big brands like Reuters, Tesco, Barnes & Noble and Toys "R" Us are well into designing their businesses so that they can complement the essential world of physical stores with a defined and powerful range of home service and online options. By doing this in a carefully engineered way they will raise the competitive benchmark for both traditional businesses and dotcoms to a level that will literally kill them. The two main causes of death will be:

- For dotcoms and unimaginative traditional businesses their costs will become hugely uncompetitive. The efficiency of their internal operations and upstream costs will fall well behind. They will then also have to react defensively and layer cost onto cost, as they bolt on a set of hastily conceived operations for online services which do not intertwine with their traditional resources and operations. Three ways to service customers will attract three sets of indirect costs and inefficiencies.
- The products and services of less organized competitors will rapidly start to look tired to many customers, who will quickly grow to expect more choice, service and convenience of access. When they get used to personal and convenient services in business travel services, or in buying groceries, they will rightly demand the same values in buying wine or furnishing a new home.

This combined effect is at the heart of the m-bomb – the multi-channel shock wave that will take the next three years to ripple out. The battleground will be seized by those major brands that we know and love, who learn how to exploit their current strengths in products and services to build cost-effective solutions for the last twenty miles to the home, the workplace or wherever their customer is.

I am sadly becoming convinced that an impressive range of established corporations will be biologically incapable of making this transition and will be structurally weakened. The good news for their staff is that the smart brands who win these wars will absorb them and will teach them the m-skills on behalf of a different shareholder.

There have been more mergers and acquisitions in the past five years than in the previous fifty years. In some ways this explosion of cost-effective and creative routes to market will represent just a continued acceleration of this huge consolidation, but for a different set of reasons.

As you would expect, I have been drawn to spend an increasing amount of time and effort working with blue-chips looking at how to survive the m-bomb. Many of the secrets, as we go through later chapters, relate to the new fault lines and approaches that we must now focus around the customer and the new infrastructures which weave the magic around today's products and services.

But I'm not just sat here doing nothing – where's the context for what I should do differently?

As a line manager in a range of businesses, I never had much time for tales of new business fashions and crises told by casual bystanders, who have never been at the coalface and who don't realize how tough the choices are for a hard pressed management team. We always have tough annual targets to meet and lots of compelling demands for resources from every quarter. Over the years we have been expected to think big and act small, empower all staff within reengineered end-to-end processes, and perhaps also to harness natural anarchy and entropy using revolutionary organizational models which humor the child and bet the business. Sounds good to me – and could I also have the red Pokémon and a French-speaking canary.

I know from my previous experience as operations director of a retail bank that most customers actually cost us money in absolute terms, and were heavily subsidized by the minority who we made strong profits from. It is often called the 20/140 rule. 20% of the customers make 140% of the profits – the other 80% really lose you money when all the costs are counted. The trick was to gradually charge the unprofitable customers for the more costly services and to aggressively up-sell them so that their profile improved.

Most normal people resent hearing about how an IT or media business has transformed its potential with a Web service or cybercafe. A blind man can see that how Michael Dell sells a PC, or how Cisco sells routers to computer departments, is of no immediate relevance to those of us who are dealing with typical customers – trying to make a buck from marketing diapers or moving specialty chemicals. The days have gone when one could lazily eject a stream of ridiculous anecdotes about Californian start-ups, who haven't yet had to deliver boringly reliable year-on-year shareholder returns. Creating stupid market valuations, which rely on being bought-out before the hard economics have to work, are regrettably a thing of the past.

In great businesses like Whirlpool or Givenchy a fabulous proposal to colonize new consumer segments, with smart-products delivered through interactive channels, has to compete for resources with investment in state-of-the-art plant, or hiring Paul Newman for $1m to spend three magical seconds talking to camera about how the product will brighten up your day.

Yes we must of course now reinvent the way that we operate – but the invention must swim up the same salmon stream as the other competing investment demands in the business.

The new marketing climate

Stock prices in old- and new-economy businesses go up and down alarmingly – based on the most trivial of sentiments sometimes.

Highly respected companies are increasingly being laid low within a blink of an eye and no one can ever feel safe any more. Great companies like Sears, Coca-Cola and Marks & Spencer are routinely accused of losing their merchandising edge and sex appeal. In a whole number of ways the multi-channel bomb ticks louder and louder each day.

In the good old days you could simply put out a 30 second ad on the TV just before Frasier and could almost call that a communication strategy, to reach the rising materialists in Chicago, Hamburg or Sydney. We all know that the explosion of media that is now taking place requires a more sophisticated, integrated marketing strategy. World masters of the m-orchestra, like Guinness and GAP, have learnt to use the paper mail, TV, magazines/print and the wide range of interactive media in much richer and cost effective ways. Just take a look at the Guinness Website to see how the content engages with the messages you have seen elsewhere – getting you dancing around your beer bottle or smiling at the oddest things. A brand leader cannot choose to ignore key communication channels like the Internet or digital TV, because new entrants can target and grab what is often a very lucrative 5% of their customer base. These early adopters may really represent 10% of the brand leader's profits within 3 years.

A hard fact of business life is that the less well-off customers are often also the more onerous ones, who place more pressure on high-street branches of banks, call-centers and returns counters in apparel stores – and who order three of everything from mail-order firms so that they can try them on before deciding which one to keep and which two to return at your expense. In business-to-business markets there are similar parallels – where smaller or niche customers can be profitable, but only when online self-service and relationship approaches are used. Businesses need to focus their resources very hard on holding onto those lovely profitable customers where the costs of multi-channel servicing and communication are affordable. If a grocery or apparel chain doesn't give their more sophisticated and demanding customers a home-delivery service or good loyalty benefits then they will lose a slice of their customer base to more "convenient" and innovative competitors. These lost customers will take with them a host of future lost sales opportunities in areas of allied needs – flowers, music, personal finance, etc.

But if you offer your expensive, added-value services and direct-marketing communications to all customers indiscriminately, you will waste a fortune – a lot of them don't want it and won't respond to it! Alternatively, if you simply stop spending your $1m on sexy TV ads with Paul Newman, and only buy signpost links on Yahoo!, you will end up between the two stools. So how do you avoid swamping all media for all customers and effectively doubling or trebling product/service development, marketing, supply chain and IT budgets?

A board who only know how to put one product set out to all customers at one price into one distribution channel, with one traditional marketing plan, should be very anxious about how to deploy a richer set of customer services without spraying a vast amount of money and management energy up against the wall. A new operating model is needed.

Introducing broader and more personalized services

In the good old days you could develop one set of products, based on technologies that you knew well, and spend money refining them and adding bells and whistles. You tried to win the award for "most versatile all-round cleaner, whilst being particularly good on stairs" or "gets the plaque off very reliably, without make the consumer choke if she swallows it." Brands did not try to stretch across to meet broader clusters of customer needs. You did quality toothpaste, not a total package of personal cleaning and hygiene products and diagnostic services to help you develop relationships and live a more fulfilling life.

The sheer cost of investing in advanced products and maintaining costly infrastructure to reach customers is driving everything inexorably down the path of diversification. Love them or hate them, but Amazon have used tools like netperceptions and their own innovation to make an awful lot of personalized recommendations, which unquestionably sell more books and increase share of household. Having spent a fortune to build that capability and all those relationships they would be silly to stop at books. It would be like building a railway which only carried coal.

People will adopt different variants and brands of products if it is made really easy for them. If handled carefully they are remarkably receptive to targeted messages and new offers from brands they trust. There is much more stretch in a typical brand than most businesses realize. If you hit customers at the right time, with the right personal offer, you can easily aim for a 30% hit on an unsolicited sales promotion, rather than the typical 2%. This is a great way to make a truckload of money and generate large amounts of shareholder value.

As a consequence, those businesses who have understood this and who have the right plumbing are all considering "mass-customizing" and extending their products and services. I could name twenty supposedly conservative household brands who are re-evaluating their options to move into new product and service areas. They will use back-office and manufacturing partners to bring in the new skills they need (such as Cotts in cola manufacturing). They will make a commercial decision whether to let these execution partners show their brand. We will hear more later on how the more innovative businesses are "hubbing" products and repackaging services creatively to give the perception of differentiation.

Everyone in the UK used to think of Barclaycard when they thought of a credit card. In the last few years no one really knows what a credit card is. For some it comes from the gas company and helps you pay your gas bill. The advertising of some cards is so strange that you think of everything except a traditional credit card. For others it is not even a revolving credit product (the professional term) because your bundled checking account handles all inflows and outflows of savings, mortgage, cash and a charge-card. For others it is a gateway to the world of discount travel and it generates airmiles. One dominant and simple branded product from yesterday blurs into a whole area of personal reward, money management and planning. Everyone can tailor what it looks like (with a picture of your pet dog Sammy carrying a scruffy bear in his mouth) and everyone can charge interest based on your personal circumstances, lifetime propensity, credit history and whether there is a hairdresser at the end of your road. Is it any wonder that Barclaycard are losing market share – and yet their service was uniquely good and everyone trusted their brand. I still believe that their services (including "lost and stolen") are the market leader, but the average consumer doesn't recognise that any more.

Be warned – your market is just as vulnerable – can you hear the ticking noise?

So let's pause for a second and draw some conclusions from all of these challenges:

1   Don't be smug about a steady stream of fluffy dotcom failures. They are not the real enemy, and when the stronger ones gang up with great brands who understand the traditional marketing, innovation and retail world they could still skin you alive.

2   The lumbering giants are now on the move and are getting into their clicks, bricks and other tricks. I can guarantee that if you knew how many missiles are in underground bunkers aiming straight at your most profitable market segments it would make your hair curl. The immediate priority is to defend your current customer base in the multi-channel game. You also need to look hard at how you can stretch your brands.

3   The brands who will survive the m-bomb will be those with an executive team and functional layers of management who are prepared to redraw the boundaries of the organization. Be aggressive in re-deploying the forces of darkness within your business to your competitors. If you don't, you will be biologically incapable of making the transition.

4   Investment demands for the new propositions must compete on a level playing field with all other demands for resources – you will need a good process to make these decisions objectively.

5   You may have been dabbling at one-to-one and integrated marketing across the different media (TV to the mailbox). You now need a far more coherent and targeted approach to the whole range of services and access channels for different customer types, or your costs will go ballistic.

6   You must challenge which operations you do in-house, in the light of the new market and the agility you will need. The new vertical specialists, e-services and technology partners who are hungry for business, can move you up the food chain, and will help you to cut costs dramatically.

In Part 2 we will address each of these general must-dos and get into the practical side of what you do to make it happen. The actions are a little harder than the words – but at least we are going where the early players have shown us the way. If you are anxious to cut to the chase, go straight to page 35.

Before we go there I have a few more forces in the market I would like to draw out.

New international competitors and marauding brands

The smart international predator brings in a set of targeted, low-cost operations with regional execution partners, which leverages their strong branding, direct marketing and service integration skills from their home market. Häagen-Dazs, Walmart, Morgan Stanley Dean Witter and Gap are all examples of smart companies who know that the opportunities in their home markets can be augmented with profitable growth in other markets. This was hard to do ten years ago, with the protected national markets, high "bricks and mortar" costs in each market and many differences in consumer perceptions, product expec-

E*Trade are a good example of a business who have a strong online proposition and who are building on success in the home market to drive rapidly for global market presence. They have used a smart approach to technology partnering – using Tanning to short-cut the process to extend the capabilities of their domestic trading system, so that they can reach ten new overseas markets within a year. The pace at which they have introduced multilingual capabilities and customized content is a great example of how to architect a business and its support systems for rapid growth.

They seem to have a very good grasp of global branding and standardization of the core offer, as well as how to weave in local "look and feel" issues which are key to success. They have a standard platform which has been specifically engineered by Tanning to support this flexible and high-speed rollout – watch out for more of these strategic platform issues later.

tations and loyalties. These have broken down in many sectors. With smart targeting the international predators can cream off many of your profitable customers, using low-cost direct channels and low-cost execution partners. Brand extenders, such as Nike, Amazon, Tesco and Virgin can find an initial foothold fairly easily. They can then use advanced relationship marketing to hunt the most profitable segments, to increase share-of-wallet in parallel needs areas (food to apparel to vacations to insurance).

The "perceived wisdom" that every Italian consumer is different to every German can be dangerously wrong, when you look at segment and lifestyle needs. They may not like the same pizza, but the professional in Milan who is going places will have surprisingly similar personal-finance and home-services needs to a similar professional in Stockholm or Memphis. Strange but true.

I am now convinced that there are very few sectors where these lucrative customer segments will not be hunted by a group of smart players, who can start by serving 5% to 10% of the market and can then ride the upcoming explosion of interactive and direct media. What concrete plans and ideas do you have in your business? Do you really know how you will defeat the economies of scale or the highly targeted approach of the entrants who have great brands behind them?

The Internet and the flotilla of cottage competitors

A swarm of cottage entrepreneurs is slowly being released as a result of all the technology and capability associated with the Internet and the new operating approaches it enables. It is also the same force which undermines the scale advantages which large businesses have enjoyed over small ones for 80 years or more. Advanced business approaches, such as using EDI for orders, billing, advanced procurement, vendor-managed replenishment and a host of other efficiencies used to be the domain of big businesses. Small businesses could not afford the fees of the parasite companies who provided the managed services (it was hard to connect everyone up to EDI – so the service parasites like GEIS and IBM had an important role). Even large businesses had to ration these advanced services to their larger customers and suppliers for cost reasons. Now the acceptance of standard ubiquitous and dirt-

There will of course continue to be many failures of new-economy businesses and these new cottage competitors. Don't forget though that 40% of new businesses fail within the first five years (according to the census Bureau). Across America 70,000 businesses of every type went bust in 1998, so you should not be overly smug about a few hundred serious Internet businesses going bust every year in 2000 and 2001. There are probably 5000 or more new-economy and cross-channel firms firing on all cylinders in the US – plus who knows how many in the minds of cottage entrepreneurs in the bath and on the freeway. For every attacker that falls you will see ten more running behind them. The *Schadenfreuden* of journalists, who have gone from excessive excitement to excessive pessimism in just one year, is masking the fact these failure rates are probably much better than with traditional capital-intensive start-ups.

cheap Internet technologies means that you can run advanced supply-chain and marketing practices into mom and pops, and specialty cheeses shops in village high streets, as well as upstream to tiny textile companies or handling agents in Korea.

Operations like 7-Eleven in Japan are linking thousands of corner stores (kochini) into advanced e-commerce supply-chains, which use the potential of the convenience store for pick-up, payment and delivery hubs. Watch out for Circle K going down the same path in the US – offering a huge range of local services via the convenience store.

An example which takes this four steps further in Europe is m-box, who can collapse online, home-shopping costs for large and small players and will add several powerful choices to serve customers in the local community as well as convenience stores (we discuss this more in a few pages). Wholesale businesses are finding opportunities to equip their tiny distributors and retailers with online supply-chain infrastructure for $20 to $50 a month or even less. What price your hugely expensive white elephant of a managed EDI service now? If you have one you should take steps to replace great chunks of it pretty quickly.

The traditional catalog businesses and many import/export businesses are all galloping to take these savings as we speak. This is e-services being used in practice at a much higher pitch than the simple Internet psychobabble. I know of a plethora of small businesses and start-ups who are forging businesses with virtually zero working capital and direct costs, based entirely upon new business models and technologies.

Giving customers choice of access and "pick and mix" convenience

Both large and small businesses can offer the customer their access-channel of choice, at remarkably low additional cost. For example, Tesco in the UK offers customers the option to walk into a store, order via PC at home or in the office or order via a mobile scan device. They have built this multi-channel capability for less than a quarter of what their main competitor has spent, in my reckoning. They do it at a fraction of the cost of Webvan. They chose the right partners (such as Unipower – www.unipower.net) and had the right vision. Add to this digital TV (which I happen to think is dreadful for high-volume ordering of things like groceries), the telephone and a games console, all accessing the Internet, and you can play tunes and choices for the different types of customer forever. I think this is great because I need never again have a fatuous argument with someone about how fast digital TV will take off and displace the PC. Let consumers vote on the different access channels as they choose, once you have engineered the main options to form part of your basic offer.

It is far easier to meet this challenge now than it was a year or two ago, because businesses like m-box are able to extend the reach of traditional brands at low cost.

A perfect example of a multi-channel service business is m-box (www.m-box.com), which has established operations in Europe. I must confess to both an involvement and a passion in m-box, because it is a wonderful mix of the old and the new – and it provides traditional retailers and manufacturers with a short cut to creating a powerful multi-channel business in just a few months.

The bush fire associated with new ways of shopping, replenishing homes and serving families and busy people in new ways will only happen when two things occur:

- There must be a step improvement in the cost of delivery to the home, so that you pay the same for everything at home as on the high street (no more delivery charges).
- A typical family must be able to order products in any way that suits them (on the doorstep, over the phone, on the PC, via the TV/WAP etc.). They must be able to take delivery in two hours, two days or go pick it up from a local store/pick-up point.

m-box has cracked both of these objectives by dragging in lots of infrastructure which is lying on the beach already (doorstep service people, warehouses, vehicles, call-centers...) and weaving them together magically with some remarkable Internet glue: the British Post Office, traditional doorstep agents (e.g. the milkmen), corner stores across Europe, the best courier companies in big cities and great multilingual call-centers and multi-channel IT players. They haven't had to build a single new warehouse or fit up a single call-center or three-temperature delivery van. This combination of existing under-utilized assets will chop the costs in half of assembling these components yourself. m-box has contracted a massive array of assets which are already depreciated, need sweating some more or are already visiting homes every day doing something else. They then use their Internet brain (called a cross-channel hub) to connect information concerning customer needs, order status and service/stock levels across all the complementary channels; to ensure that someone like my mum can order the brands she loves on the doorstep, change the delivery time on the phone, track the order on the Web and pick the case of wine or MP3 player up at the local store on the way home. All at no delivery charge from the retailer.

m-box is a multi-channel service business, which gives the manufacturer and retailer a wide choice of ways to reach their customers – complementing the high-street relationship and keeping their brand in the foreground. The call-center agents work around the clock, answering the phone using a customer relationship script which will "live the brand".

The Website would also of course be strongly branded as the manufacturer or retailer, but with a little m-box logo in the corner to reassure the consumer that everything will happen when it is meant to, and with a customer experience that provides all the new choices to the home. An e-fulfillment equivalent to "Intel inside".

New service businesses like this for the last 20 miles mean that you can implement new multi-channel strategies very fast (three to four months) with very little up-front costs. Your competitors can beat you to this powerful new service by spending as little as $300k to setup and $10 or less per fully serviced delivery (multi-channel IT, customer-care and delivery). The eagle has landed.

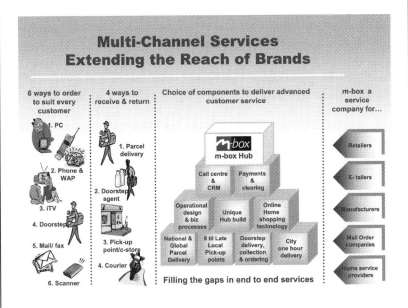

Fig. 1.1 Multi-channel services extending the reach of brands.

Who cares if only 10% of your customers order on the Web, as long as those that want to can do it with you, rather than leave them to shop in a more sexy or convenient way with Carrefour or Home Depot because they have made it possible and you haven't. And those that choose your more expensive services who aren't profitable can be charged for home-delivery, unless they have a mortgage with you, or take your travel insurance, or have 2000 loyalty points. This, in my view, is how companies like Walmart will move from 200 million high street customers to 400 million customers in the home, high street, anywhere.

When Toys "R" Us had the vision to partner with Amazon to manage their "last 20 miles" it is no surprise that they galloped rapidly past eToys. They had the brand and now they have the short cut to the full multi-channel range of services.

Broadening the offer and extending reach

Businesses that have designed themselves for multi-channel operations can also then easily bundle their services with those of other complementary product e.g. chocolates, flowers, wines and hampers can be assembled really easily to take the hassle out of organizing a party or a picnic. At very low cost, a wider proposition can be offered to customers in any region where the product and service can be delivered reliably. This is a far smarter and more viable approach than those silly Websites which just try to sell you chairs or candles. Not many people in the real world ever just want that – they have wider needs and they would never have the time to mess around shopping in such a piecemeal way. If you want to protect your margins and solve customers' problems on their terms you need to help them clean their homes, replenish their larder, plan and manage their finances or help them move house. This is why initiatives like the Transora exchange, which involves all the major FMCG manufacturers, could be such a powerful force. On day one they will focus on purchasing savings, but the medium term options include all the consumer-goods businesses getting together to offer a carefully chosen range of totally new home-service or lifestyle offers direct to the home – cutting out the retailer to some degree and protecting their margins. How could Kmart or Carrefour hope to de-list all the big brands if they decided to extend their reach all at the same time?

Why everyone needs a good strategy for the new channels

To close this section on the difficult terrain that lies ahead, it is worth dwelling briefly on a few anecdotes from the market, some of which ask some enthralling questions.

The challenge for many manufacturers and product businesses is how to avoid upsetting their current outlets and retail partners when

Proctor and Gamble and Heinz both have smart responses to this potential threat. P&G launched a service called Reflect, together with some smart partners. They offer personalized cosmetics to suit your individual tastes – made to your own "unique" specification. This new joint venture is not offering the same range as they put through the food retailers and the drugstores etc. so they avoid the headbanging with Walmart. They can safely learn a lot about individual consumers and their preferences and they get an award from me for being particularly smart. Good proposition, good personalization, good channel strategy, good avoidance of the retailing bear-trap – good job!

Heinz have done even better. They offer their direct retail service of "brands from home" to expatriates. Using this clever model there is no chance of a product being offered in competition to the local store (because expatriates are only ordering products from home that they can't get locally). An expatriate living in a distant plague-ridden land will pay almost an infinite amount to avoid their baby having to eat something that may kill them. Further magic and brand loyalty is then created from the fact that they maintain the link with products that they miss from home (strong emotional plus rational needs are being met). Heinz use international parcel delivery to get the goods there – a very cost-effective and reliable execution. Expatriates also have a high propensity to use the Internet, so the fit and preferred access/ ordering channel with the target audience is great. Wow! Great proposition, no channel conflict, great learning, highly segmented, lifestyle/loyalty enhancing, makes money, good supply-chain – brilliant!

they go direct to the consumer – not as the endgame but as another way to serve and connect with the consumer.

Consider Home Depot's dilemma, who allegedly have been robustly discouraging their suppliers from selling direct on the Web. Black & Decker or Bosch could easily put together a fairly useful online power-tools shopping channel or hiring offer, which cuts out the middleman for the more informed customer and builds a two-way dialog with the loyal customer. Retailers like Home Depot will usually threaten manufacturers that if they sell direct they will de-list them. That attitude smacks to me of a retailer who has no confidence in their service and probably no imagination in terms of how they can add value in the broader service they offer. I would probably use this zero tolerance approach as well if I was in their shoes, but I would only use it as a stalling tactic. If it happens to you as a manufacturer you have to deal with it sensibly of course. The "closed shop" retailers who forget the laws of "evolve or die" will inevitably get complacent and find themselves outflanked and out-thought. It will work out well for them in the end, as long as they don't hide behind the defensive threat strategy forever.

Now why can't we all think that way?

Please don't underestimate the value of a service like this one from Heinz. When I lived in South Africa I would sometimes sit on the step of a hut in the bush and listen to the sounds of the wild – a black-backed jackal calling for her mate, the cicadas chirruping away happily and the clink and clank of the cooking pots in the kitchen area. As the sun started to set over the fever trees I would see a fish eagle swoop down through the crisp amber landscape. Just as it extended its claws down to snatch at the water's surface a hippo would gently rise out of the water behind it and yawn. Vast pink mouth, stubby white teeth and an image that would stay etched on the brain for a lifetime. I would sigh, sit back in my chair, and dream of a pint of Brakspear's. For those Philistines who haven't heard of it, this is a beer that is brewed in Oxfordshire in England. This beer has touched my senses and my spirit at so many important moments of my life that I would pay ludicrous amounts of money to gain access to it in strange places. I would then also be certain to consume it in great quantities – as would my friends and acquaintances who would be infected by my romantic loyalties. Chocolate has a similar effect on my personal assistant, Larraine. When I bring her some little chocolate eggs from some friends at Cadbury's she can't resist popping one in each cheek immediately – like a demented hamster. What price or value a proposition such as Heinz's, if one extended it to all products that travelers could be longing for? Anything an expatriate or tourist may crave. What value can you put on convenience and long-term loyalty for the chattering classes?

We can now add a few more calls-to-arms to our earlier ones:

1   There is no long-term future for the one-size-fits-all offer. You need to become adept at bundling products and services differently for different sets of customers. These skills and infrastructures will be essential to protecting your current profit streams, as well as providing you with the means to become a brand predator yourselves – deepening the offer and moving into adjacent areas of customer need.

2   Many small local players will be successful in developing strong multi-channel franchises in niche areas, but the big games will be won by those with global leverage in R&D and product innovation, customer management infrastructure, media skills and international partnerships. The bureaucratic national and regional conglomerates who treat each national market separately will struggle badly.

3   The Internet-based technologies and exchange services are equipping cottage competitors to use the same advanced business and marketing/service approaches which are available to the big guys. It is quite possible that the historical scale advantages of being able to afford EDI, SAP etc. may now become a millstone. Large businesses have to move on and find other scale economies or their overheads will strangle their competitiveness when compared to the cottage players.

4   We are now within reach of "access channel of choice" becoming the norm. The best businesses are engineering their operations so that customers can have five or more choices of ways to browse and order, three or four ways to receive the goods or services – from

high street to doorstep and from PC to TV. The entire economics of home fulfillment and multi-channel ordering have finally changed in the leading markets.

5   Multi-channel and tailored services will be used by many businesses to cross-sell, up-sell, refine the offer and give customers some types of added-value that weren't possible before. Propositions which look logical from a customer standpoint work well – those that are product-centric often don't. Invention and the right sales processes can produce extraordinary profits, as well as new services which are genuinely practical and earthed to the needs of customers.

6   Channel conflicts between manufacturers and retailers will come into sharp relief. They center on who owns the consumer and whether retailers will allow manufacturers to move from supplying products to supplying services. In the end the market and the best propositions will win, but only where the players have clearly thought through how their different offers complement each other.

Part 2

Planning Your
Multi-channel Defenses

In Part 1 we hopefully laid to rest the ghosts that can prompt businesses to dismiss the new channels and e-services as a flash in the pan. We have all seen a good selection of ill-conceived new-economy failures, but they still represent a lower failure rate than with traditional start-ups.

It is becoming easier to separate the white noise of fluffy Websites and silly consumer propositions from that gently building ticking noise which is coming from the sleeping giants and the credible new players who are marshalling their forces. We have illustrated where the real threats are coming from and have also drawn out the capabilities and broad thrusts that are needed to survive and prosper in this more complex market place.

In Part 2 we will go into the specifics of how businesses must reshape themselves so that they can develop the new services, offers and customer operations that they will need. We will also introduce the types of practical strategy that they must choose between. Time is short and the costs of choosing the wrong path through the woods will be hugely expensive.

I should also stress that the extension and transformation of a great traditional business should be a whole lot of fun and a very challenging and rewarding activity. This is as long as the leaders have enough humility to recognize that they must use their best judgement to build the right strategy and operational platforms, but also that they will then need to let things evolve in the white heat of the market. No one will know all the answers and a great deal of rapid iteration and fine-tuning will be needed.

Let's go deeper now into how you define your strategy and how you can reshape a traditional and successful business.

Chapter 3

Conceiving the Multi-channel Organization

If you are driving a traditional business and you want to go multi-channel and extend your basic service proposition then there is a lot to be done quickly. As in family life, the conception stage can be the most fun of all. It just happens to have more urgency about it – if you don't get your act together in tackling the m-bomb you will face death by a thousand cuts, as new entrants hunt down many of your most profitable customers. The key is to keep your costs at a competitive level, while you move selectively to stop new entrants from offering your customers enticing new services which you cannot match. I can almost guarantee that you must move more quickly than you are used to.

To do this you must exploit the power of the new approaches and infrastructures quickly, but with a ruthless focus on what your customers will find useful and what will save you money in your basic operations. We will talk in the next chapters about the various defensive and offensive strategies that you can adopt. But I have found with almost every business that I work with that there are a handful of golden rules which shine through the fog every time. In my view, every business that will compete effectively in this new marketplace must look very hard at the principles that we have drawn from all the early success stories.

Principles to die for

Before we start talking multi-channel strategy we should go through a

12-point health check for your current business strategy. This can help tell you how prepared you are for the m-bomb.

From our experience the following principles must guide you as you urgently change your business to respond to the market forces and opportunities that we discussed in Part 1:

1 You are not starting with a blank slate. *You must quickly start to remodel your current business operations around an updated understanding of the needs of your customers – across traditional and new channels.* Underlying and emerging customers' needs are the only driver you can trust to earth how you set your priorities. This will become clearer later, but it is a hugely important operational principle and it is not a shallow platitude. If you forget it, you will lose your way.

2 *You must differentiate your products and services to meet the needs of individual customers or broad customer segments.* This is, in essence, a 'mass customized' vision for standard products and services, but with individual interaction used with each customer to give a genuinely personalized service. Very few businesses can handle the operational complexity of serving more than six to eight general 'types' of customer, in terms of prices they will pay, charging that you must apply in order to be profitable, channel choices they will want, added-value offers and loyalty approaches they will respond to. You must effectively create a 'pen-portrait' service for these high-level segments, which all your people understand and buy into – you must be able to treat customers differently at several levels. We provide examples of these 'pen-portraits' in the next chapter.

3 *Leading businesses should aim to be first-movers in their own sector, but should be fast-followers in terms of global Internet and multi-channel innovation.* The new access mechanisms, supply chains and customer-management processes do not differ so much from the retailing of books or personal loans in Germany, to cars in the US. If a company can pick up and exploit approaches from other geographies and sectors they can short-circuit a huge amount of learning. You have to be very stupid in this fast-developing market if you refuse to learn from the experience of others.

4 *You must spend almost equal energy looking inwards to use e-business approaches and innovations to find cost-savings and efficiencies from your existing operations. This will help fund the new investment that you must make.* In my experience this is almost always possible. A change program which just focuses on the sexy business-to-customer benefits is usually a bad sign – there should be a good cost-saving balance also. Most businesses have high back-office costs and usually have several separate projects duplicating key infrastructure. Stop building expensive capabilities that you can buy in.

5 *The executive team should critically challenge the ideas which are on the table.* There is no reason for company boards to passively accept fluffy learning initiatives, which will never make a profit. The Internet is not a discount channel and anything else you do should not be either. Most of the normal business rules apply – they are just interpreted in some new ways. Just be careful that you don't mistake a swan for a duck, through lack of experience or historical prejudice.

6 *Never pretend that you know exactly where all this is leading and that you know precisely how customers and markets will react. Be a little humble and be prepared to adapt. For this reason you must typically drive projects that reach the market in four to six months. You can then scale up towards the ideal.* Generally speaking a $500k project is better than a $5 million one. You can see so many businesses getting this wrong, as they commit $10m or move on long, slow and highly orchestrated investments, which head off doggedly into the fog.

7 *You must plan for some very quick wins.* They will build confidence and in every business there are always at least three visible and easy-to-measure quick wins to be had. If you can't find high pay-back opportunities then you aren't looking properly. They are in the first wave of your multi-channel and e-services plans. Having spotted them please do not spend six months then debating the blindingly obvious!

8 *Don't mistake the Internet for a set of technologies which is only accessed by personal computer.* There is no war between digital television, the Internet and the high street or the sales force. They are all channels which customers may individually choose to use.

They operate at different levels in a multi-channel jigsaw – doing different jobs. However, what we refer to simplistically as the Web is one of the powerful glues that helps integrate these channels into an efficient and low-cost set of services. These serve the customer in whichever way they choose to deal with you on any given day. If you don't understand this principle and design your business around it you will die gracefully. The key activities which serve the customer must operate seamlessly across both existing channels and those that are emerging. This is not a recipe for everything being neat and tidy and purist though. Nothing will ever be tidy again.

9 *Think of your customers' needs in a broader way than you do at present.* For example, don't sell them a car – solve their total transportation problem. Anyone with a powerful brand, great customer knowledge and a mastery of e-services is a potential early competitor, so get your retaliation in first. Look at your customers' needs for convenience, one-stop servicing, added-value information. Walmart can attack Best Buy's market just as easily as Carrefour can move into retail banking and attack Crédit Agricole.

10 *Whenever you talk to or touch a customer you must show that you understand them.* For sales and relationship-management purposes this must include what products they are most likely to need, as well as the details of your products that they already have. This ability to demonstrate intimacy, and ensure that sales offers are always relevant and meet real needs, must be deployed equally in face-to-face contact, online services and occasions when they phone you (or you phone them). This can be relatively expensive to build into your operations in just a few months but it will become a competitive norm within three years. So get on with it.

11 *You can no longer expect to influence your best customers through mass-market advertising.* Even yesterday's version of integrated marketing is proving to be simplistic, where a new formulaic letter was mailed to customers every month or so. You must improve how you co-ordinate and target sales offers, brand-building and service experiences differently for the various customer types you are trying to reach. If you don't you will soon fall behind customer expectations for personalization (they will see what the likes of Amazon can do and expect you to do the same).

12 *You must benchmark your costs against the emerging leaders of the multi-channel game and react to mismatches very aggressively.* Some of the advantages of scale will continue to exist for another few years, but many of the more important competitive edges are being eroded before our eyes (procurement, advanced stock-management approaches (EDI) ...). The Internet and the new broking services which are coming together are slowly 'democratizing' many of these previously expensive and advanced processes. If you were starting again you would set up a business with a fraction of your indirect costs and using a lot less capital and people.

Please use the 12-point checklist above to do a quick health check of your current strategy and plans. Try it to see how many of the twelve principles you have built into your existing plans and can tick with confidence. If the answer is less than eight you should panic (and fire yourself and your strategy director).

I use a variant of this checklist to analyze what I can see in the market to pick stocks for my modest investment portfolio. I have huge confidence that these fundamentals will win through – whether the overall strategy is cautious or bold. The important point is to operate consistently by the principles as you develop your plans.

The essential competencies for a multi-channel business

If many of these skills and infrastructures are new then it follows that you may decide to spend less time on traditional competencies, particularly those which customers don't care so much about or which all your competitors do just about as well. It is lunacy to think that everything can be done in-house to world-class standards. Moving away from yesterday's core competencies is always a painful business and is usually very upsetting. But unfortunately you do need to be brutal about how you can really differentiate what you offer now. The focus of your internal management effort has never been more important.

To repeat ourselves a little we can now turn these ideas around and bring the challenge for today's successful businesses into sharp focus. You must build an organization which can:

If some of your key staff are uncertain about changing focus I would tell the story of what Terry Leahy of Tesco said a few years ago about banking in the UK:

"What Tesco found was that customers had not really understood financial services as traditionally offered to them...

"They found the location and opening hours of the providers were inconvenient...

"What they wanted was convenience, simple products, good value and good service...

"They were open minded about who they got them from."

I was responsible for operations and IT in a large retail bank at the time. We had to respond to this challenge, so I remember the piercing accuracy of his words and their potential implications for our business. I recognized at the time that he was right and I think the success of the food retailers entry into retail banking products has proved him right. You should pause briefly and consider whether any of these sentiments would be applicable to your business (change the words "financial services" to "surgical support equipment" or whatever it is that you do).

- *Reach a customer through any new channel or interactive access device without additional operations or systems* (PC, Smartphone, call-center, Sega console, $40 hand scanner and bar-coded recipe in a magazine ...). Can your IT department tell you how they could take an order from a customer or salesman which has been sent via a Sega Dreamcast or portable Internet device? If not, then ask them to get with the plot.
- *Bundle new products and services dynamically.* If you can structure yourself to bundle products, information and added value in simple but impressive ways, your customers should be able to see a rolling wave of service innovation without too much new R&D heat and noise.
- *Extend customer knowledge and intimacy to new areas of need without significant new cost.* By working with partners you should

again be able to integrate more powerful propositions for your customers. For instance, retail banks can offer small-business customers a total package of business administration, online trading and communication infrastructure, rather than just simple banking services.

- *Continually strip out duplicated processes and in-house services which benchmark badly.* Always know who is doing call-centers, warehousing, back-office admin or procurement most cheaply and effectively and be ruthless about demanding those services and costs for your customers. For example, if you are still running your own call-center I suggest that you go for psychotherapy. It is a misleading old wives tale that you cannot use third parties to touch your customers in ways which ooze your expertize and values – many internal call-centers are amateurish and very poor value for money. Even little things like communications services can be overlooked year after year so they become uncompetitive. Web-based international phone calls are now a penny a minute – what are you paying?

- *Compete on service rather than price.* Progressively improve the customer and product mix, with targeted communications and services. Anyone who competes only on price in the new service channels is either paying to secure share in a poorly served market or is very dumb. Customers who contribute most to profits will always pay for services that they really need.

- *Succeed and fail much faster* (with less sunk cost) and then build upon your successes rapidly. If anyone suggests a two year project you must send them for a good lie down.

- *Restructure easily and rapidly, as the market and management require.* If your current organization or processes are a barrier to changing aspects of your organization every six months then you will struggle to stay competitive. People who continue to moan about constantly changing organizations are missing the point. The only organisms that will remain static are dead ones. Change should be no big deal.

In my view, there is no business of any size which can afford to ignore these challenges. From our experience with many leading businesses around the world, and quite a few new ventures, I believe that the bulk of these new capabilities can be engineered within three years at most. Businesses which go down this path will be much the better for it, even in terms of traditional customer reach and commercial measures. When you add in the real multi-channel gold rush, beyond the false dawn of the Internet and the new competitive benchmark, you will create a shareholder value equation to die for. If you can link a strong traditional brand and skills with these capabilities I would predict, as a ridiculous generalization, that two thirds of your competitors will be biologically incapable of making these changes happen. It is not that hard to do – if you can think, walk and chew gum at the same time. The trick is to display sufficient humility, so that you gradually cement these more flexible operations while you listen carefully to the changing needs of your customers.

Now the next two chapters are a little heavier – they go deeper and talk about what this all means in more specific terms – redesigning your operations, choosing your strategy and learning from others. I would suggest that before you get into this you get a cup of coffee.

If you prefer a lighter spell first, you could go instead to the good, the bad and the ugly (Chapter 6) or to the gentler but vitally important 'getting it done' topics in Part 3.

Chapter 4

Building the Customer Operating Model

The customer operating model is the single most important operating infrastructure that a modern flexible business can build. If it is implemented correctly, you will have all the defences you need to survive the m-bomb and to go on the offensive in new service areas.

Let us remind ourselves why we need a more customer-focused approach. In most sectors I believe that current services:

- are not convenient
- are not well understood
- are not enticing
- are not tailored/personalized
- are not priced according to real service costs
- are becoming undifferentiated
- are inefficient, compared to greenfield entrants and agile competitors
- are poor value for money.

This is largely true of banking, luxury goods and travel worldwide, but I would suggest that it is also true of most retail operations and a good proportion of service businesses.

What has caused this to happen?

It is not because businesses are intentionally offering poor service. It is because they have kept offering variants of the service that was feasible ten years ago. They have not reinvented internal and customer-facing operations to reflect the potential of new business models and communication technologies.

Interestingly the opportunities to offer a lot more value and convenience to customers are often obvious to new entrants, but they present great emotional challenges to traditional companies. Companies like Virgin found air travel, financial services and cola to be very soft targets – and the response from the incumbent players has been quite slow really. Established businesses tend to have entrenched views on how to resource and optimize their business the old way, so the new service offers and ways of working are harder to see. I find it fascinating that businesses like Virgin can be so innovative in looking after customers in Financial Services but so able in my experience to get it wrong in other areas – I have a personal story to reflect this lack of attention to detail.

I was on an interesting train operated by Virgin in England about a year or so ago, travelling from Manchester to Birmingham. It stood out from other journeys in that their unique technical problems behind the scenes managed to turn my expectations of a pleasant travelling experience to a perception of being part of a hostage situation. Yes, OK, it was a joke really – but a travelling stranger and I (a visitor from New York) developed a highly plausible hostage theory to pass the time and to explain an increasingly implausible sequence of events.

The engine on this relatively short trip had to be replaced three times in the space of a hundred miles or so. What was meant to be a quick journey became punctuated with the grunts and groans of engineering failure. A boring and repetitive commentary was maintained by "Simon" on the intercom, telling us about the latest position as he saw it and occasionally heralding the solution which he felt was close at hand. The following example of Simon's energetic delivery is not verbatim, but is close enough. "We are stopping at Stoke to change engines. We are sure that this will be the last time and will fix the problem, which is a technical problem of some sort. We hope that you are coping with the delay as well as you can. We would like to apologise for any inconvenience." He was no doubt using some sort of script, but was routinely unconvincing and the information was always devoid of real content. Mysteriously, no one was getting off or on as the train limped along between engine changes and abortive attempts to fix the breathtaking array of technical failures.

The tale of disaster and ill-informed comforting continued. After an hour or so the passengers actually started to smile and talk to each other – a most unusual thing to do on an English train. My new American friend who was sat opposite me started to conjecture that the train may have been taken over by terrorists and that negotiations were clearly underway with the authorities. Between us we rationalized all of our experiences on the train with this theory. We were obviously being fobbed off with increasingly ridiculous and vague excuses to mask the real situation. For the next two hours there was not a single piece of evidence that this ridiculous theory was incorrect. The Virgin staff were so ill-equipped to manage the unfortunate sequence of events and they kept accidentally using Pythonesque language and overtones, adding to the mood of gallows humour and mock hysteria.

One of the ironies in first class was that we were right by the engine. We could hear the engineers/mechanics talking loudly about "the thing is just held together with sticky tape" and "I've rigged it but it won't last long." You knew that the droning voice of Simon on the loudspeaker was unconnected with the unguarded voices of those who were trying to cope with a succession of old or poorly maintained engines which had been inherited from British Rail.

Things will always go wrong in complex businesses, but if you don't equip and train the staff to "live the brand" and co-ordinate the customer's experience in everything you do, then the customer will never forget either Simon, or what we perceived as the serial incompetents responsible for the engine. Living the brand is about distilling what you offer and stand for into the right staff behavior and service for the customer, through almost any set of circumstances. This is not usually about free drinks or ridiculous apologies, but about equipping staff to anticipate what customers may need at each stage in the service and, if things go wrong, what they should expect from you in terms of professionalism, anticipation of special needs and honesty. The customers who have "off-brand" experiences, even once, will typically retreat from being potential advocates or just thinking "they are all the same aren't they" to spiralling into becoming contemptuous of the company's broken promises in their marketing messages. An informed and highly competent response to failure will create advocates. The reverse destroys trust at an alarming pace.

My tenuous respect for Virgin's brand continued to slide a few weeks later when a friend told me that his Virgin train ran out of petrol – apparently a cardinal sin for a railway, which may signal risk-taking with customer service or plain galloping greed. Petrol stops cost money, so unless someone forgot to replenish the tanks there are apparently only pure cost reasons to cut it fine, given the huge impact on customers. As a slightly disgruntled customer, I didn't even think to verify whether my friend might have been mistaken, or challenge what he said. The point here is not whether he was recounting his experience accurately. It is that I was now ready to believe the worst of Virgin rail, because the magic of the brand had already started to wane for me.

Shortly afterwards Virgin then started, in my opinion, effectively to force all "customers" on the Birmingham to London express in first-class to eat breakfast, as our fares increased by around £20 for the trip and the meal was "bundled in." Many fellow passengers immediately complained to the staff "I just want to work. I don't want all this breakfast rubbish on my little table! No I don't want a cooked breakfast!" (subtext – I am tempted, but I will put on 15 pounds if I eat a fry-up every day and I will lose working time). They effectively forced me to pay for something I don't need but I hate to see go to waste. What brand value does cluttering your workspace, and pre-charging you for tempting fattening food fit into?

The most criminal mistake in this off-brand rail journey was that if you don't travel first-class you don't face all these dilemmas. This is an excellent reverse example of a differentiated service. Virgin have systematically put at risk their relationship with some of their highest potential business customers, who also may be the most profitable customers of Virgin Atlantic. The icing on the cake was again the staff, and how I experienced them initially distancing themselves from Virgin. A customer would complain and the ticket inspector would answer loudly, "Yes I know. I get an awful lot of complaints like that madam. It doesn't suit people who want to work on the train, but we think that 'they' will change back when they hear the complaints." It is the same story as before – service innovation or price-management appearing to gallop ahead of staff training, not to mention customer needs. You cruise into your destination to the strains of "they think all forms of transport are an airplane," as they pass round hot towels which a few people accept fairly dutifully.

At the other end of the spectrum we have American Express, whose service when you lose your credit card or have it stolen is legendary. A chat to one of their "lost and stolen" staff is an object lesson in staff training, attitude and "living the brand." They gently talk you down from your anxious state, they will contact anybody for you to get help – they go the extra mile. Their basic credit-card service is expensive, but when things go wrong you soon learn what the brand is about. They have also woven together their services across the channels so that the call-centre, the mail and the burgeoning set of online relationships will keep as much of the personal touch as they can.

To help you build new customer-centric services there are a range of new partners you can look to:

- Specialist call-centre players like Brann in the US can handle telephony and broader customer-care services at lower unit costs and with much higher functionality than most plodding in-house services. It is all they do and they do it well. In Chicago, Illinois, they have a call-centre with staff who allegedly have 26 languages. Brann, Merchants or 7C in the UK employ highly educated people and they can take an incoming service call and turn it into an intelligent sales offer using a script better than any internal team could do. This is not about commitment. It is just a reality of specialization, focused investment and strength in depth.
- The connectivity of good customer relationship database technology and middleware systems such as Siebel, Netperceptions, Broadvision and Shopping-magic can create multi-channel supply chains and levels of personalized services that companies could only dream about a few years ago. Many companies still mess around trying to build bits and pieces themselves, or trusting to SAP to solve it all in five years time with mySAP.
- The best of the new e-fulfilment businesses can now handle all the home-service issues – so that the last 20 miles can be managed with the same operational values as the high-street operations.

In the rest of this chapter we will see how an established business or new entrant can structure their business to deliver reliable and cost-effective service, which can:

- Create an integrated operational design that will supply and service customers seamlessly across both existing and new channels. Customers should be able to contact you by post, then phone you to continue the dialog, and then complete the transaction or enquiry in a store or via the Internet.
- Introduce profitable new propositions and services, which targeted customers will find enticing (and they will perceive to be logical extensions of the current services).
- Provide different levels of service for different types of customers – retaining and attracting the most profitable and lucrative customers.
- Provide a cost-effective way to offer customers self-service choices (change my order, open a new account, check options and book it), and an increasing level of personalization.

Steps required to define your customer operating model

To introduce the customer operating model, there are some simple steps to go through.

1   Define your high-level customer types or segments

For each broad segment you will need to understand:

- Which channel the customer prefers to use for their most important interactions with you – e.g. preparing orders, taking delivery, solving queries and problems, paying for the service.
- Their likely response to intimacy or personalization of the offer. Some segments respond very well to relationship services, which treat them as individuals in the way that sales offers are made, e.g. I will set up the overdraft – but if you would like a loan for twice this sum it has already been approved for you. Just click here to activate it (30% of customers will say yes – believe it or not). Other types of customer hate this "contrived" intimacy and hate being sold to overtly. My father is one of the latter. If someone tries to offer him a service he hasn't asked for, he will say no on principle,

and hate them forever for intruding on his space. Other customers will never order on the Web so long as they draw breath and can dress themselves. They may actually order from someone who is supported by the Internet – but they don't want to know that!

- The relative profitability and status of the customer. This will be key to choosing how much you will invest in the relationship and what choices and services you will offer the customer. Low-value customers are likely to be charged to use high-cost services and will not be offered added-value services e.g. rare wines at auction or exclusive tasting sessions in the local store.
- How likely the customer is to be interested in new services and products in adjacent areas of need e.g. travel offers, wine-cellar management, en-primeur purchases.

You should try not to define more than six major segments which you can build services around. These integrated views of "customer types" will help enormously to get your marketing, sales, operations and commercial people talking the same practical language and agreeing how you will develop propositions and serve different customers in the future.

There will of course be a more sophisticated dialog at a personal level with your customers, which effectively treats them all as individuals. But if you don't "mass customize" your core operations and services your own servicing problems and costs will go ballistic. A good high-level segmentation is the very stuff of life which will give shape to your operations, systems, staff training and product innovation. You can also see hopefully how the broad segmentation can be readily turned into procedural scripts for the call-centre, face-to-face staff and for online servicing e.g. if they are a high value customer then offer them this, or waive that charge. It is worth noting that there is always more work on the operational design and training side than in the IT – but you can imagine the customer delight that you can generate. Most importantly you can then treat customers consistently and appropriately – which they care about very much (remember my Virgin story).

We call these m-maps! Multi-channel maps which help you to segment customers and then plan how to service them (and structure the underlying operations and systems).

The reason that competition will be getting stiffer for every manufacturer and retailer is that these segment models are getting much more similar across the sectors. The more sophisticated food retailers are finding that the needs they are naturally homing in on are very similar to those of general retail, and even financial services or travel and entertainment. If you gear up your business to deal with your key customer sets in the more rounded and convenient way, you will find it much easier to both retain your best customers and to sell them other lucrative services, which your neighbours think are their preserve.

To bring this approach to life, it is worth looking at the typical thumbnails for customers in financial services and wines and spirits (Figs 4.1 and 4.2). You will notice that each box takes a view on the questions that we asked on page 50, e.g. which channel does the customer prefer to use? are they receptive to new propositions?

Which segment do you fit into?

Try to position yourself and a handful of cousins and aunts in your family. It is often surprising how neatly a wide range of typical people you meet in the street will drop into segment models like these.

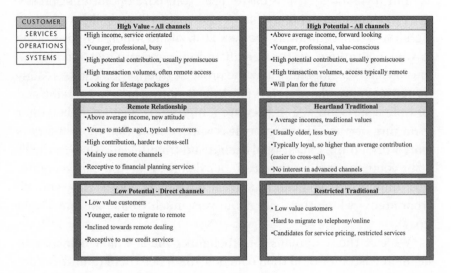

Fig. 4.1   Customer thumbnails for financial services.

Fig. 4.2 Customer thumbnails for wines and spirits.

Let's now look at how a wine and spirits spin would work. Notice how we are deliberately forming a view on how each segment would respond to the key service issues which a multi-channel wine business would need to factor into their servicing plans (who would respond to holidays in wine areas, who needs advice on what to buy, which is the primary service channel, what is the likely profitable potential and status …?).

These are slightly sanitized versions of the real thing, to protect the innocent. We have found though that the segment models are remarkably similar between companies which have a well-developed understanding of their customers (and who have researched service needs as well as product needs). The trick is to rapidly develop your initial four or six thumbnails and then to research them using pragmatic approaches (e.g. use focus groups and then introduce pilot services of the new personalized services and channels – see the P·R·I·C·E Approach™ in Chapter 7).

As you gain operational experience of offering new services to customers and treating them in these different ways, you should use your practical experience and customer feedback to modify the thumbnails, and keep track of how the different customers needs are developing. The thumbnails will never be a perfect picture of your current and target customer base, but they will force you to understand their generic and specific needs more accurately and to differentiate your service to them. If you want to speak to some masters of these clicks-and-bricks services you should talk to companies like Merita, a Swedish bank which has been online and multi-channel for 15 years, or Gall & Gall in Holland (wines and spirits). Gall & Gall have developed an excellent model for building a home-shopping service on the back of a world-class retail offer on the high street. Their store managers keep these sorts of segment models in their heads. The human brain is still one of the best customer-relationship databases in the world.

2   Now define how your services will be delivered across the channels for these segments

The first task now is to pick out the main interactions that your customer relies upon and values the most. In our financial services example below this is broken into:

- Simple and frequent transactions such as getting cash and paying-in checks.
- Other basic services, such as moving money between accounts, changing address details and requesting statements.
- Opening and using simple products, such as savings and loans (known to a bank as a simple sales process, but to the customer as a flexible facility and offer, which is available when needed).
- Making decisions about, and then setting up, complex or regulated products such as pensions – these require advice and a more complex execution process.
- Personal financial and household planning processes, which are typically self managed and operated directly by the customer using a PC. The more established companies are introducing clever products and services in this space – including personalized healthcare, education and other long-term planning options.

For each key process you need to decide which access, servicing or dialog channel you think is most relevant and affordable for each customer segment. To help illustrate this approach we have included a generic servicing map for financial services (Fig. 4.3).

A lot of garbage has been talked about the Martini proposition (anytime, anyplace, anywhere), where a business will offer all their customers every service through every channel. This is a very expensive way to run any service, because you layer cost upon cost for every single customer, without necessarily increasing sales. Providing a customer with three ways to talk to you is always more expensive than providing just one route. Low-profitability customers should ideally be migrated over time to low-cost servicing channels and should be charged to use more expensive retail facilities, home services or customer-care operations. I instinctively dislike this discriminatory approach (having starting life as mildly left wing and socially aware), but as I grow older and drift gently towards fascism, I see the commercial necessity of doing things this way.

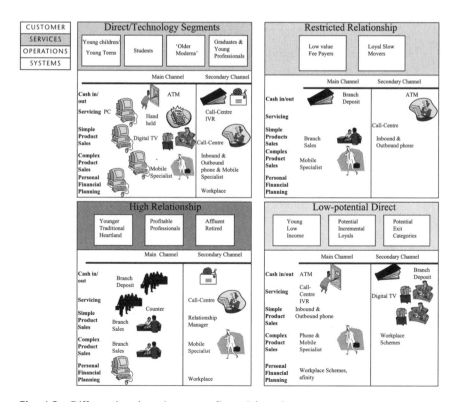

Fig. 4.3 Differentiated service map – financial services.

Customers who frequently use your loss-leading discount coupons or special deals and who buy few high-margin products from you can become a waste of time and effort. You only have so many servicing resources, promotional dollars, staff in outlets with time to talk and expensive staff in call-centres. Why on earth would anyone trying to make a buck give the most profitable and the most loyal customers a diminished share of that scarce pool of services and support resources?

My advice is to think very hard about how you can gear your operational choices and promotions to your best customers. If you

It is worth looking at some of the forces that drive consumers to use online channels for the first time in different countries. It is often not for commercial reasons – sex and sport drive behavior still. A Spanish-backed operation behind the 'Big Brother' TV program has apparently been using a special voyeurism format to drive the mass-market towards the Web. The programme involved locking a whole bunch of people in a house together for a few months and putting cameras on them 24 hours a day. The programme bombed in the US, but in most European markets the formula of watching a weird and wonderful group of self-publicists living, loving and laughing, minute by minute in real-time proved to be very compelling.

The Italians I think got the record for the quickest on-camera sexual encounter, and in the other countries the voting of who should leave the house each week captured the public imagination.

Throughout the weeks and months, a live feed was maintained to the Internet – and more Internet virgins went onto the Web to spy on their antics than for almost any other reason in 2000, particularly for the non-English speaking nations. Having broken their duck for basic entertainment reasons, some of these consumers will now move on to book their vacations online and a range of other things.

A number of smart people will continue to work out how consumers can get driven from one channel and service segment to another. Sex, sport and entertainment are not the only triggers – but they do work well sometimes!

don't know who they are then for heavens sake find out. Similarly, you must not ram the Internet down the throats of valued customers who prefer to deal face-to-face. By implementing a smart multi-channel customer strategy, which serves different customers in different ways, you will save millions in operating costs and will also be able to delight your customers in different ways as you move them up the profit curve.

But how do you reorganize your product and servicing operations to plug and play across the customer-base and the channels in this way? How do you achieve what FedEx effectively achieved all those years ago – opening up their internal product handling, ordering and tracking operations to customers – and a whole lot more?

You need to redesign your internal operations, without losing the value of all the investments you have made in the last thirty years. This is not about slash and burn, or finding huge sums of money. It is about using the Internet behind the scenes to unleash the potential of what you currently have.

3   Implementing "plug and play" customer operations and supporting broader propositions

The broader propositions are the new and more profitable ways that you now will use to package and sell your services. You are typically bundling other services around your basic offer – for example:

- You used to sell cars – you now provide cars "built for me" with flexible financing options, best insurance "for me," best breakdown and recovery deals, peace of mind GPS and mobile phone packages to keep me safe, etc.
- You used to sell mortgages and current accounts. You now provide powerful cash- and loan-management facilities for me – tailored to my needs right now. You run your old separate products behind the scenes, but I see my personal net-worth summaries and planning options on demand. You automatically move my cash around in the best way for me and you help me to manage my long-term affairs, without making me feel conned and bamboozled. I am in control but I value what you do on my behalf.

- You used to sell me groceries or pharmacy products. You now provide my everyday needs in the home in a way which is most convenient to me. I can pick things up or have them delivered, whichever suits me today. I can buy cleaning products or you can organize my house-cleaning or laundry for me. You don't do everything yourself, but you guarantee the quality, and fix it if my service doesn't come up to scratch. I also like to get one regular delivery at home – rather than twenty different parcel operations all bringing their specialist products on different days.

Introducing the product and customer hubs

To deliver these broader propositions it is always wise to view things with the customers' eyes – to link things together using the logic customers would use. Then you need to be able to "hub" or package the different product components together operationally, so that the customer has one integrated way to order, enquire, complain, arrange deliveries, get a price, choose their product/service options, etc. This is supported by the customer hub, as illustrated in Fig. 4.4.

The product hub is a magically easy information switch and utility, which will package new services at very low incremental cost.

In the high-level operational design shown below you can get a glimpse of how this works in financial services, using a combination of internal and third-party services (without the customer knowing or caring). Below we show a business-to-business example (see Fig. 4.5). The product hub is a set of support operations and information systems which collect and aggregate underlying information seamlessly for the customer. You interface them with your existing back office, manufacturing, logistics operations and those of your partners.

> Apparently, the only services which have remained completely unchanged for the last 300 years are prostitution, beggary and a small number of rural crafts. The list of services that remain unchanged for just the next five years may be almost as short! A product hub will be key to those businesses who are looking beyond prostitution or beggary.

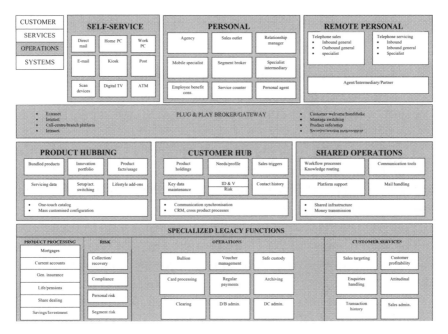

Fig. 4.4 Customer operating model – financial services (generic version).

The customer thinks that you have created a wonderful new money-management service, which reports all your finances together in one consolidated statement. Actually you have just assembled all the balance and transaction data from the old operations and put them together in a sexy new way, online or on paper. You have also co-ordinated new product improvements and information servicing using an internal intranet – so that you can keep it all stepping forward in the eyes of the customer.

This is the operational level of the **m-maps**, which help structure the business to serve the customers in the intimate way you need to across the channels. The operations staff in the business need to ensure that they can operationally detach the specialized functions from the hubs and the interactions with the customer-facing channels – so that they "plug and play" together in this flexible and powerful way. This is the key to being able to bundle services together in the eyes of customers. If nine different divisions have all these parts of their operations coupled together tightly, with their own unique product processes and big chunks of the customer-service infrastructure are duplicated, then you had better move very fast. You will never deliver cross-channel or bundled propositions at anything like a sensible price.

We can see a similar model for business-to-business (Fig. 4.5).

It would be way too boring to go into detail about every part of this operating model – but you can hopefully see the logical separation of back-office and partner stuff, customer-relevant and supply stuff and channel-delivery options.

Forget scrapping your old product operations – just reinvent what you offer your customers in terms of how services are packaged. Then separate, de-duplicate and recluster your key operations, based on the new service design.

Capital One were reputed to have churned out 14,000 products in one year. They seemed to have created a system which scaled up the 25% which worked and canned the others, without too much ceremony.

It is essential also that you forget building all the new skills and competencies to do this yourself – just find some good partners who have the bits of the advanced proposition that you are missing. Some of your divisions may contribute key chunks of this "plug and play" model. Other operations will be too dysfunctional or archaic and will need to be replaced. This is often where start-ups find it easier – they know that they can't do everything themselves. So they find the best

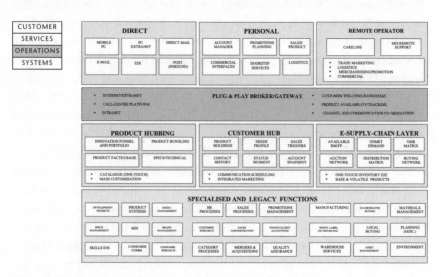

Fig. 4.5 Customer operating model – B2B and retail channel.

capabilities in partners, hub them together and get to market in four months. Some brain-dead businesses hate the idea of using partners and spend years trying to gradually remodel a cow into a gazelle. Meanwhile, groups like Walmart use GE to manage and finance their card operations – and look at the speed that they can move at.

There is also no point in waiting for "the new enterprise IT solution" such as SAP to be implemented across all your operations in three to five years time. Many of your most profitable operations will be half-dead by then. If you can build the product hub in 6–12 months you can move your business forward rapidly, to assure your long-term flexibility and competitive response.

However, you will never again be in full control of all product delivery components – and neither should you want to be.

Introducing the customer hub – an infrastructure for the next ten years

The second side of this operational revolution is the customer hub.

The customer hub operates using similar principles to the product hub, but with a different purpose. It aims to give your customers the experience or perception that:

- You know the important things about your entire relationship with them, i.e. every product you have sold them, where they live, how they like to pay for things, what they have just written to you to complain about (and they are now phoning you to follow up).
- You do not insult or irritate them by asking them for things which one part of your organization already knows (how often have you been asked in application forms for your name and address, when you know the company already has that information?).
- You know which services will appeal to them and which they probably need next. This is based on their lifestage, gaps in current product holdings or purchases and status. You make these offers at smart times, but very gently and in a way which is easy for them to say "yes" to.
- You know how they prefer to deal with you – which channel they like for browsing, ordering, touching and feeling, and asking for advice. You know how their channel preferences are likely to evolve

for some products. They still like coming into stores, but will top-up or repeat purchase online.

- You value their loyalty and reward them differently to a customer who appeared yesterday. There are many ways you can show this appreciation, without resorting to crude discounts. You can further influence buying behavior in smart ways and can drive substantial gains in "share-of-wallet".

- You ask them for identification, special dates and personal information only when you have a practical use for it. You never ask them irrelevant research questions.

Customers are already learning to value and "love" companies who treat them in this way. There is evidence that they are starting to dismiss and even despise companies who can't be bothered to get to know them and serve them well.

In time gone past the customer hub was occasionally found between a traditional salesperson's ears. We are now going one step further and guaranteeing that the knowledge in the sales guy's head, and all of the other customer information we have, is available automatically at every point where we touch the customers. Customers love to be known, respected and treated appropriately – as long as it is not done too intimately and disrespectfully. The key of course is to assemble and deploy customer information very smartly and sensitively, and to adapt operating procedures and staff training to maximize the impact on loyalty and sales.

The operational customer hub should be developed rapidly, to give all direct self-service processes to customers (Internet and smart call-centre) and provide relationship and support staff who deal with the customer with the tools to treat the customers in this new way.

Your existing systems will be fine for managing the operations behind the scenes. They just need to be linked via the hub to exchange information, as every order is taken or completed and whenever any contact point learns something important about the customer. The new operational design for the key customer operations does take a bit of work to introduce, but it can usually be brought together effectively in six to nine months.

If anyone on the operational side says it can't be done (or should not be done) then please fire them immediately and find someone more creative who has a passion for serving the customer in richer ways.

For the world that is now emerging this is one of the most critical things to do this year, whichever sector you operate in and whoever your customer is.

Don't forget also that many partners, agencies and brokers can be engaged to talk on your behalf to your customers. Don't fight against this or you will be forced to acquire too many in-house skills. Just make partners adopt your relationship model, use selected aspects of your hub data (which remains your property) and ensure that they exhibit and display the values of your brand. The chances are that they can recruit better multilingual call-centre staff than you can or can build a better information service – but never forget who owns the relationship with the customer.

The electronic supply-chain layer

Each business will also need their own specific "end-to-end" operations streamlined, to operate at low cost across the various channels. The Internet technologies can be very powerful in rapidly linking a number of internal upstream and supply-side processes with the processes which customers see, e.g. to transform the complete catalog production cycle or to reduce cost and improve communication in the whole manufacturing and stock management cycle.

A great example of this is what I call the "electronic supply-chain layer," which can use ubiquitous Internet technology to virtually eliminate certain types of inventory, working capital and availability problems from the supply chain. The Internet has been a godsend in providing a low-cost way of taking EDI techniques and vendor replenishment up to a totally new level.

The principle of hubbing is used again here. All operations and processes which touch product inventory should tell the "inventory/ demand" hub, which sits on the intranet/Internet, whenever they see demand from customers, when they move stock, when orders are placed on suppliers and when stock is produced by the factory. Many clever terms are used by suppliers for the same Internet technologies, but effectively they can all link suppliers, procurement brokers (e.g. Ariba, efruit, e-conomy, transora), logistics partners, factories, warehouses, distribution centres, retail outlets and online ordering systems.

The growth of procurement exchanges will be an interesting case study to watch over the next three years. There are currently 658 exchanges being incubated in boardrooms and cafes across the world. They are designed as buying clubs which companies can join, to gain access to the best deals available due to the combined purchasing power – you too can stand on the shoulders of giants. In the second phase they will go beyond quick wins like this to reducing trading costs through advanced common processes and Internet technologies, or even cutting retailers and intermediaries out of the entire supply-chain. Companies will first club together to cut raw material and supply costs, and will then look at how they can start beating up on anyone who is between them and the end consumer.

If you put any four graduates in a room for two hours they will come up with the opportunity to set up another exchange. They are easy to conceive, offer the prospect of early hard savings and they lead to loads of other superficially compelling destinations.

What is actually happening is that we are only just beginning to understand how to screw up exchanges – and are a long way from understanding how to make them work. By the time this book is published you will probably already see the first wave of failures, where the first fallers will demonstrate the nightmare of developing consensual approaches, in committee, negotiating at the pace of the most stupid or power-crazed person in the room.

Standards committees and consortia have suffered from these problems since the dawn of time.

The exchanges who don't have strong participants who also own the exchange will have the other problem – where the big boys are half in/half out, mess with the standard specifications and lose a lot of the scale synergies.

The great news is that a next generation of benignly autocratic and free-play exchanges will emerge from the rubble of the first wave. They will go under another fashionable name and approach, but they will get to the Promised Land. Please don't let the imminent failures and underwhelming experience of the sunrise days put you off the substantial opportunities, lying in the deeper currents flowing along behind these new e-services business models.

Shallow but promising innovation comes quickly with the new economy – more fundamental seismic shifts take a little longer and are often built using the wreckage from the first wave of hits from the m-bomb.

Whether or not you are taking 10% savings in raw materials from these exchanges you can also make a lot of headway all by yourself. The most advanced businesses and the smarter start-ups are now effectively creating a one-touch stock-management and call-off system, using regular Internet technology and security processes. These services don't care which system or company/customer is accessing them at any specific time (so long as they are certified). Let me give you an example from leading players in the catalog sector, which would typically be used for selling apparel.

Inventory items are classified in three ways. They can be held as local stock items, called-off when ordered or made-to-order items. The consumer or local ordering agent will start the process by seeing the lead-time for non-stock items. They are then offered delivery slots which factor in the ordering or build lead-time. You may not always get "now," but you do always get certainty! The only permanent stock in the system will then be the stock which manufacturers or Far East supply agents decide to carry on consignment or at their cost, to organize efficient manufacturing runs. Other stock in the supply chain for these classes of product is simply that which is in transit to the customer (or is held in returns). Suppliers, who can't operate using these new ordering, delivery and track-and-trace infrastructures are either de-listed or retrained/re-equipped. Forward-thinking businesses may also supply these infrastructures to the agents in the Far East or the local distributors, so that they are locked into exclusive partnership arrangements on advantageous commercial terms. It is amazing how many businesses and import/export agents in India, Hong Kong and Singapore are now connected to the Internet, with this in mind.

Kumars are putting 50,000 VSAT-connected Internet terminals into more than 1000 towns and villages across India. The local trading network will exploit these links in a range of simple ways. The international supply options will open up dramatically. Countries like India and China can pull a lot of manufacturing output away from the factories in the developed world, if the logistics can be streamlined and the communication lines shortened in this way.

Everyone benefits from these virtually inventory-less processes, which can be implemented in a matter of months and will deliver huge savings in customer response and in the overall costs of doing business. The big difference in direct supply chains is that many customers will happily share cost-savings and receive a product in ten days at a lower price, rather than pay for all that unnecessary inventory and handling. You don't learn that from the current retail model! Don't think for a moment that all customers want to pay for one-hour delivery and unlimited availability of product ranges that never change.

The only expensive class of stock is the evergreen or big seasonal items, which are ordered forward in bulk for efficiency reasons. The retailer or distributor must then market the hell out of these products, using a piece of the virtual or personalized catalog which is planned well in advance.

Many of today's leaders in the catalog businesses are locked into a costly and highly inflexible 9- to 12-month cycle, built around a paper catalog and long-term supply commitments (with largely one class of stock). *The new Internet-based model represents a genuine revolution, which explodes the opportunities for flexibility and up-to-the-minute merchandising and will inevitably cause a bloodbath for moribund suppliers and retailers.* The good news for existing players is that we see a number of start-ups losing the plot here also.

The next stage of the electronic supply chain is then to use the reverse auction model to say to haulers and suppliers – I have these orders coming in – who can do the best price for me next Tuesday? Try this and watch the price, cost and administration improve dramatically.

4   Systems to make it all work

We show in Fig. 4.6 how a typical systems architecture will support the new channels and the new customer-operating model. This is potentially a cure for insomnia or a stimulus for repetition, given the business background that we have just gone through.

I should just point out four things that your IT people must buy into (and many already have probably):

- SAP, Baan, Peoplesoft or your 20-year old integrated system must be coupled to the foundation of the multi-channel architecture. The customer and product hubs and the message broker/switch which you see in the architecture are the keys to leveraging your business skills and resources, across any access channel your customers may choose. If you don't have a light, fast and intelligent message switch, which spans all of your customer-facing operations, then how on earth are you supposed to put the same service out in both face-to-face and online channels (without huge double handling and IT)? How can you hub customer information if your insurance service or enquiries service is directly coupled

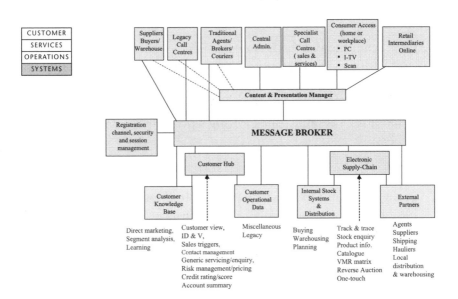

Fig. 4.6   Typical target architecture for multi-channel businesses.

to the standalone back-office system? You must build in a general customer welcome and recognition process before you go into the specialized product operation.

- *A telephone, a hand-held scanner chained to a catalog in a store, a digital TV, a Playstation games console, a PC and a mobile phone are* all *Internet access devices.* A call-centre, a terminal in a shop and a mobile system used by a sales rep are similarly just a few more access channels into your business (via the message broker). For those who hate it when everything seems to be new, let me just say that the message broker, the hubs and many of the back-end systems can run really well and quickly on *mainframes* (and often better in large businesses than on the cheap and cheerful stuff that Gates produces). But that is just a reassuring detail for the old timers.
- The key to the architecture is that all front and back-end systems must be enhanced to "plug and play" together within three to six months. Your only main problems will be if the technical interfaces to your very old systems can't be tailored easily or your data models are terminally incompatible.
- The business change and behavioral change to make all this work is ten times harder than the IT challenge – so for heaven's sake get this IT bit planned and scoped quickly.

We have again showed the financial services example for consistency, but architectures in other sectors have many similar characteristics.

So let's sum up some headlines which will help you to reshape your operations around the evolving and individual needs of your customers:

- You must question how convenient and enticing your services really are. Think about whether accessing your products and staff is easy as 1-2-3. Can customers help themselves? Have you opened up your product knowledge, planning systems and ordering systems to them directly?
- Make sure everyone in your organization knows how you are planning to serve different sets of customers in different ways. Ensure they use the language – this offer is for the "high service

A small example of something you need to plan for is the powerful growth of online communication via e-mail. E-mail accounts almost doubled worldwide during 1999. If the trend continues we will have higher global penetration of e-mail than TV by 2003. It is surprising how few businesses are engineered to exploit these ubiquitous 'simple' access channels and technologies, which are now integral to the lives of staff and customer alike.

rollers," but we expect to catch a few "heartland cliff-dwellers." It is OK to use a bit of humor and attitude in your mass-customized multi-channel thumbnails – but only go for four to six at first and don't let the customers know how you classify them!

- Don't think that everyone wants to deal with you online or on the phone. Some do, some don't. Others will always want a face-to-face contact – if you can afford to provide them with one. To do this, however, your costs could explode, unless you restructure your product infrastructures and services operations around product hubs and customer hubs. You don't need to go into all the boring details of this yourself – but you do need to ensure that your operations and IT guys get with the plot, using the top team's priorities and milestones.

- Learn how to bundle products and services imaginatively, using partners here and there. You can then offer the market a continuous flow of new products and benefits without needing to do too much fundamental innovation.

- It is amazing how much a "pick-and-mix" multiple investment product can feel like an incredible innovation to a whole bunch of typical customers.

- Ensure that your people can say "mobile, store, digital-TV, PC, whatever – it's no big deal now. Our operations are geared up for any access mechanism the customer wants."

- Broaden your product offers to include bundled services, which your research tells you the customers will respond to. Don't sell insurance – offer a financial planning and security service. Learn how to manage every risk in the home and find the partners who can help you deliver the proposition. Learn to partner as if your life depended upon it. Learn that you can't do everything in-house, but that you can co-ordinate what the customer sees.

- Front up your stock, manufacturing and buying operations with an Internet supply-chain layer. Do it in six months. Tie in to the procurement exchanges also, but don't panic if it seems futile at first.

- Find a "get it done" set of IT and operations partners to build e-services and architecture into your core infrastructure and services. Of course you must get integrated and drive the big changes, but it shouldn't cost a fortune and involve slash and burn.

So is it right that we have just decided to develop your business so that it can foster multi-channnel services, customer innovation and significant cost savings, before we have even settled on the broad strategy for the organization?

That is no mistake of course. The precise strategy you choose will influence your priorities, and does need to be discussed in the next chapter, but what we have just covered is about creating the leanness and fitness you will need under any scenario. None of these broad thrusts we have just discussed is entirely optional, for all sorts of defensive and competitive reasons.

These changes are needed to survive the m-bomb. But you now need to decide how much you will be leaping tall buildings in the new landscape, or how much you will be thriving by foraging in the forest using fairly familiar skills. Let's talk strategy (or if you find strategy too dry or want to visit it later, jump directly to Chapter 6 instead).

Chapter 5

Strategies to be
the First Brand Standing

It is easy for a large and complex business to agonize over the type of strategy that should be adopted. Every business has an existing set of product, customer and regional strategies which have evolved over many summers and winters. These now clearly need to be adapted to fit the new competitive landscape. As we know from the framework in the previous chapters, a new set of performance benchmarks and capabilities, and a range of new organizational models is now possible. Many new competing demands for resources are looming, and yet the old pressures for investment still apply.

For many companies it feels like it is time to pause and to spend a few million on a root and branch strategic review. There are so many options to consider – much to ponder and much that we need to know before we move ahead. Let us dabble with a few experiments on the Web. Let us ask good old Sam, who is free at the moment, to mastermind some tactical things, while we stand back and commission a big consultancy exercise. We need to know if the dotcom bubble has really burst. Perhaps it might come back.

Please don't do this. Life is too short. And you have only just finished the last strategic review which you are still trying to make sense of. There is another way. A way which puts your house in order, and gets you on a strong evolutionary path that is going in the right direction.

In my experience, of doing this with a wide range of companies, there are three types of basic strategic direction which come out of modern strategic processes. Remarkably the options of "life, the universe and everything" to build a multi-channel business can be distilled into three broad paths. From Guinness to GAP to Walmart you can see how they all drop into these three simple strategies. They all tend to rely upon not digging up bits of road that are freshly dug and working OK. They all focus to varying degrees on the customer-centric, multi-channel and e-commerce cost savings, which represent the 80/20 that almost any company should be able to go for.

So what are these three options and how do I go about choosing which one is right for my business? How could I possibly ensure that a generic approach could be enriched and tailored for my particular situation? How can these possibly fit almost any sector?

Everything which is simple usually conceals a lot of complexity. Let us now see how the options really work.

1 The "create the platform" strategy

This path is a highly successful and realistic strategy for many types of traditional businesses. It focuses on moving the existing business towards the shape of organization which can exploit multi-channel operations, but at a measured pace. The emphasis is on securing substantial initial cost-savings, rather than making too many changes that the customers will see immediately. There should of course be many indirect benefits for customers, which are at the heart of how you get it right for them and keep your prices competitive.

Objectives of this strategy

This strategy can be summarized as:

> "To provide one-touch operations and infrastructure for customer services, stock management, order processing and sales processes – to generate cost savings, enhance flexibility and transform supply chain relationships. By doing this, open up the business for future electronic access channels and tailored customer services."

I use onion charts to show very simply how these strategies play out (see Fig. 5.1). The "aim" explains itself. The "be best at" layer then picks out the most important things you have to be great at for the strategy to be successful. I guess it is obvious that the competencies that you don't pack in here are inevitably less important in the new strategy. The "major thrusts" in the outer layer are the "must do" 7 or 8 activity areas or operations which will be needed to make the strategy happen. You don't pluck these things out of the air of course – you need to pick out the aim that is right for the business as it heads for the m-world, and then work through the new skill areas, "be best ats," and the consequent action areas or thrusts to get there. The onion chart puts a whole lot of thinking, strategy and action onto one page – so all can see the focus of strategy, skills and action.

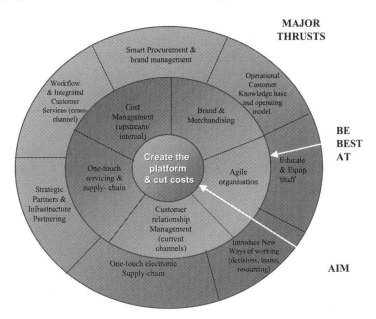

Fig. 5.1   Create the platform for multi-channel operations.

Success for this strategy is measured by:

- Retaining existing customers.
- Avoiding easy wins and impact for new entrants.

- Getting cost out, to meet a global cost benchmark.
- Staff able to understand and see the benefit of e-services and "clicks and bricks."
- Securing the best fulfillment and service delivery partners.

The onion chart (Fig. 5.1) shows the ingredients of this strategy. Any strategy statement which is easy to define must always be translated into a set of hard implications, which tell you how the strategy will help you to compete and what you need to do to execute it successfully.

Emphasis in this strategy is placed on servicing the existing customers better, using primarily conventional sales channels and media i.e. this is primarily a retention and cost-reduction strategy.

If this isn't ambitious enough for you I would suggest that you jump to the next one on page 77.

Implications of the "create the platform" strategy

Many smart companies choose to follow this type of cautious but highly intelligent strategy – it keeps all their options open and it secures some important cost savings. If you go down this route you will do the following:

- *Setting aggressive cost-savings targets,* which force you to implement right-first-time resolution of customer queries, advanced procurement approaches using low-cost Internet approaches, automation of many admin functions and outsourcing of activities which don't differentiate you, and which others can do better or cheaper. It is still good to use start-ups as a benchmark – to see what they outsource to keep internal baggage and assets low, and flexibility high.
- *Creation of a powerful, flexible and transparent electronic supply-chain service,* which initially serves the internal and upstream (supply-side) supply chain. This low-cost set of Internet services will sit above your existing systems for warehousing, shipping, planning, call-off etc. Each underlying service or system is configured so that it tells the Internet broker what has been

moved, shipped, been broken or ordered – all in low-cost real time. This approach should reach every supplier you use (or you stop using them), every agent/broker, every stock point etc. In many businesses the product innovation and merchandise selection chain and the catalog/range processes must also adopt a similar philosophy and infrastructure - with huge cost and flexibility benefits. It would be too boring to spell this out more fully – but your operations and IT people should get it.

- *Simple workflow processes will be implemented across all customer access points,* e.g. field sales, call-centers, retail points etc. This infrastructure supports the "one-touch" or right-first-time approach of answering a customer inquiry, processing a customer's written complaint or prompting a salesperson to sort out a problem using one coherent workflow system.

- *Implementation of an operational customer hub or database* that provides the essential customer information to the primary contact channels – supporting the goals of customer retention (intimacy), increased sales penetration, and again the one-touch approach to customer service. If you talk to a customer in a friendly and knowledgeable way they will buy more products from you. Trust me – it works.

Key competencies

These major thrusts are designed to generate efficiencies and build or reinforce the following competencies which you will stand or fall by:

- Integrated marketing – touching customers efficiently and consistently across direct mail, TV, online and radio etc.
- Customer relationship management (the ability to serve traditional customers in the intelligent and informed way that they are starting to expect from the best businesses).
- Advanced supply-chain operations and IT integration (at a working capital and flexibility level that you could only dream about two years ago, even with full EDI).

- Innovation in day-to-day customer service for existing customers (e.g. loyalty processes, streamlined administration, personalized service).
- Product innovation – this has never been more important. It will remain the basis upon which you compete.
- Cost control – meeting new entrants head on and advancing ahead of plodding traditional competitors.

If prioritization is to mean anything then the other less important competencies should have less call on management and financial resources. Please don't waste money on installing a sexy new asset register – it won't frighten your multi-channel competition one bit.

Benefits of the strategy

It will become increasingly apparent as you follow this strategy just how fundamental these apparently modest thrusts and competencies are. They are key to creating an effective platform to bring in new customers and in moving to new ways of servicing customers with enhanced propositions. The great thing is that this strategy pays for itself many times over, almost from the beginning. I have seen major cost savings from these right-first-time and one-touch processes and services. More interestingly, you should look to obtain a sales uplift of 20–40% from existing customers. This results directly from a more automated and knowledgeable sales offer – made at the right time, in the right spirit of intimacy and as part of the natural servicing process.

I would summarize the benefits and disadvantages of this strategy as follows.

Benefits

- Increased customer retention and penetration (integrated marketing).
- Improved internal efficiency and substantial cost reductions.
- More productive supplier relationships and procurement flexibility.
- More responsive product development and range management.

- A strong platform for future customer e-services and advanced operations.
- Low operational risk.

Disadvantages
- Potential strategic risk (fast enough? radical enough?).
- The internal changes can be expensive and can hit inertia.
- May not attract new customers, or retain early adopters of new channels.
- Generates limited learning from new services and customer demands.

From my vantage point I would say that companies like Guinness and Nestlé are typical adopters of this type of strategy. Guinness are spending a lot of money building a highly competitive platform for their businesses, which will position them well to move quickly and efficiently across their most important territories.

One of the most common concerns about this conservative but highly profitable strategy is that you can still be outflanked by an aggressive competitor. They can transform the market or entice your best customers away. This is a definite threat in markets like financial services and healthcare, where the service is generally such poor value for money. Such services can be very impersonal, and hard to engage with and understand. They offer low perceived value for most consumers. Some businesses will want to look for a more aggressive path, which focuses a little more on growing the top line and your market share. So let's check out the more aggressive range of strategies.

2   The "improve the proposition" strategy

This is a great path for many consumer, retail and premium business-to-business organizations. It puts many similar pressures onto the internal organization as in the previous strategy, but it puts a good-sized toe into the water to test the emerging needs of customers who are looking for more innovation and convenience. It involves a strange mix of a bit more risk and a bit less risk, at the same time. More risk of biting off a bit more change. Less risk in trying to adapt the internal organization, without knowing more about the customer's reaction to the self-service world of the Internet and the new channels.

Objectives of this strategy

The strategy can be summarized as:

> *"Use internal cost-savings to fund the extension of core services and relationships. Exploit these capabilities, channels and skills of partners to acquire new customers and profit streams."*

The onion chart in Fig. 5.2 shows the implications of this strategy.

So what are the implications of such a strategy?

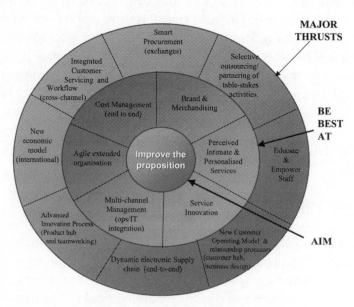

Fig. 5.2 Improve the proposition and the customer service mix.

The battle will be won or lost based upon the ability to retain existing customers and to attract a targeted number of early adopters, using both traditional and online media and sales channels. Success will rely upon finding the right partners in key areas of service and adjacent propositions (e.g. bundled insurance, online content). Only the more imaginative and agile companies should go down this path.

If you go for this type of strategy you will do the following:

- Set aggressive cost-saving targets and create the electronic supply-chain service, as outlined earlier in the platform strategy.
- Introduce customer-segment managers, who would aggressively recruit profitable new customers, using existing and online channels. These relationship managers would define the product and service propositions needed to attract these early-adopter customer types.
- Develop customer-centered operations and workflow activities which span traditional channels and online services (PC, new access devices etc.). In IT parlance this is often called middleware, where one co-ordinated set of services for product, pricing, promotions, account maintenance, delivery scheduling, payment and customer identification serves all the channels (call-center, online, retail and sales staff). This is achieved by using one integrated set of systems and processes behind the scenes. An operational customer "hub" is then able to actively co-ordinate these sales and servicing processes across the channels, as directed by the customer segment or service managers.
- Develop a simple product hubbing approach, which would allow more advanced and rounded propositions to be offered to customers. This may be more of an integrated reporting and "packaging" of separate operations, so that you look and feel far more innovative. It may represent some genuinely innovative new services, which change the market fundamentally.

Key competencies

The core competencies that we are trying to build and reinforce here are:

- Customer service innovation and relationship management (with different types of customer being treated in different but appropriate ways).
- Advanced supply-chain operations and IT integration (including advanced manufacturing and logistics tendering).
- Customer service and product innovation (product and service bundling being a particular learning priority).
- Multi-channel management (delivering a coherent set of personalized and self-service choices to customers, across online, telephone and face-to-face operations).
- Service efficiency and cost control initiatives, e.g. back-office automation, employee benefits services via the intranet (outsourced), travel services etc.
- Brand building and communication, so that the new propositions can be heard and will get share of voice in the white noise of the new media. This will often involve signposting online services via traditional retail or doorstep channels (if you order via the Web, I will ensure it gets to your house on time – or you can pick it up here on your way home).

Using this strategy we go further in building the platform for multi-channel operations and broadening the offer. A serious start is made to recruiting new customers who will help us to better understand the needs of these emerging segments.

Benefits of the strategy

This strategy is again fairly self-funding and it balances risk sensibly, by not overestimating demand for direct online services.

This strategy also enhances the innovative attributes of the brand – both in the eye of customers and shareholders (which is no bad thing given how share prices ebb and flow based upon the most trivial of old and new-economy sentiments). The strategy raises barriers to exit for high-value customers.

I would summarize the benefits and disadvantages of this strategy as follows.

Benefits
- Significant cost and efficiency savings.
- Strong loyalty potential.
- Flexibility to drive profitability of different customer segments – and to focus servicing choices and costs towards profitable customers.
- Good defensive strategy for early adopter customers (existing and new).
- Platform for brand extension and new propositions.
- Realistic expectations of adoption of new channels (only 5–10% of customers will use the new channels and services).
- Good potential to generate shareholder value.

Disadvantages
- Higher cost and risk – places more bets on the new channels and propositions.
- Can still be outflanked by radical competitors and new entrants.
- The market-facing initiatives may distract energy from internal efficiencies.
- Significant management and competency stretch.
- Expensive new skills are needed (returns, payments, distribution, product bundling …)
- Significant infrastructure costs/risks.

The grocery multiples in the US and the UK give us a great example of this type of approach. Walmart and Tesco are pursuing the early adopters, using convenience and extended services with gusto. They are not forgetting to squeeze every ounce of cost-saving and efficiency in the supply chain also.

A real favorite of mine in this space is Gall & Gall – the traditional wine and spirits retailer in Holland. They hold 25% market share as the dominant player. They are a lovely business populated by lovely people. I am biased because I have worked with them, but you have to be impressed by how an "old economy" market leader can launch a best-in-class online home-shopping service from scratch in five months – soup-to-nuts. A supposedly sleepy Dutch retailer, who has every reason to be complacent, has combined the old and the new in a way which puts most traditional and many start-up businesses in the shade. They also have a sophisticated economic model which tells them precisely how they can make money from their multi-channel services. Gall & Gall have learnt how to use the Internet to extend and enrich the customer's relationship with the store – rather than to undermine a relationship with an arid online service. They have also been able to block competitors moves and new entrants very effectively.

A variant of this approach is called "partnering with a live wire" or "doing the three legged race with Carl Lewis." The Toys "R" Us link up with Amazon for home fulfillment achieves some of these results, without them taking risks with their in-house operations. Great Universal Stores in the UK bought Jungle.com for $50m, and inherited a great online electrical and technology/games retailer, to complement their traditional home-shopping services. The real test now is whether Jungle stays as a fancy but separate online division – or whether they can reverse-engineer a true multi-channel operating model across their whole business.

The third and most radical strategy is either for the bold or the seriously wounded (which is more of the world's businesses than one would expect).

3 The "change the market" strategy

This strategy is only right for businesses which have a good amount of ambition, cash, adrenaline, and which serve the type of customer who will benefit significantly from a more rounded set of propositions. It is obvious to me that selling books, holidays and mortgages fit this category, whereas this is less obvious for purveyors of garden products or pets.

Objectives of the strategy

The strategy can be summarized as follows (see also Fig. 5.3):

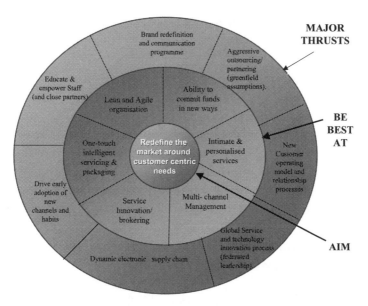

Fig. 5.3   Transform the market.

"Transform the market for our brands and products, around a more rounded set of customer-centric needs and greater tailoring of service. Increase share and economic value dramatically by being 'first mover' – drive the market."

With this strategy you aim to be best at:

- Partnering with other businesses which can extend your proposition, in order to meet a wider set of needs or to generate strong new revenue streams.
- Personalized communication and relationship management – without which you become invisible in the dog-eat-dog world of interactive master brands, rampaging across the sectors.
- End-to-end cost and service management – integrating the full range of advanced services and partner services, to ensure that the customer experience meets the customers' expectations, at lowest cost in your market.
- Driving existing customers to these new and more convenient or rewarding services.

- Product and service brokering – you don't own it all, but you must deploy it all. This is a tough and unfamiliar skill and will require you to make the selection and integration of partners a core competency.
- Multi-channel service and quality management – forget a best-endeavors service level with new channel operations. Most of the early online shopping companies thought they could get away with pathetic delivery options, which occasionally delivered Christmas trees for Easter or would frequently expect the customer to wait in all day for a delivery that never arrived. Early surveys found 80% of customers suffered from stock shortages, delivery problems or ordering hassles. An online service needs the same operational values as a traditional retail operation. Customers need to be informed and in control, every step of the way.

This strategy majors on targeting the fastest-moving and most lucrative customer segments (usually internationally), reaching the most critical clusters of unmet needs in adjacent product areas, e.g. from grocery to videos to dry cleaning to full home management for busy people. Both traditional and new media are used co-operatively, to drive customers to migrate to the new service propositions.

Implications of the "transform the market" strategy

Typical initiatives would be:

- *Creating a dynamic "plug and play" electronic supply-chain service* which would extend seamlessly to partner products and services (remember the examples in Chapter 4).
- *Setting cost-saving targets and acquiring fulfillment partners* – to provide cost-efficient services which can be woven into a more responsive and scaleable set of operations. Acquiring execution partners will often involve the transition and disposal of in-house operations, which can be better managed by partners, e.g. call-centers, logistics and IT operations.
- *Creation of customer-centered operations* – not just the customer hubbing, but with service hubbing also. To allow totally new needs

to be met, e.g. "I want to move house", rather than "I want a mortgage" (see Chapter 6).

- *Aggressive realignment of the marketing proposition and brand* to reposition a new set of services in the eyes of the customer. The product and service boundaries now stretch to meeting whichever sets of basic needs the team identify as extending value significantly. Convenience and personalization becomes a fundamental part of the value proposition, e.g. "I can reach this service anywhere in the world and they know what I want before I do myself."

To bring this strategy to life I would love to use a number of recent tales from the market which I know so well but which are still confidential. One that we can talk about is EMI and Musicmaker (www.musicmaker.com). They have together decided to transform how music is bought and listened to by all of us. You make up the CD by choosing just the tracks that you like. Why is it that two-thirds of the tracks on every album are fine and the rest are boring or just plain offensive? You love the first track but the second is brash and tuneless. At last you can make up your own favorite Springsteen or Elvis Costello tracks, and download them to your MP3 player from the Web at the same price as the old standard CD.

We can relate this to our strategy implications for the "transform the market" approach. A new electronic supply chain is in place, particularly because the product is also electronic. The marketing proposition is aggressively realigned and the brand now redefines what you think of as an album. Your fulfillment operation uses new online distribution partners rather than high street stores. The customer hubbing, and the way the retailer can know your tastes, will allow personalization engines to profile your musical taste so accurately that I am sure they can pattern match you with other similar consumers. If you like slower Radiohead or Stones tracks, then the more advanced profiling engines can predict that you are bound to love quality Cabernet Sauvignon from Chile and scuba diving in Grand Cayman. I am rambling a little to illustrate the points – but you can see how a "transform the market" strategy can build rapidly alongside the traditional market and can rapidly kill it off in certain extreme cases.

Key competencies

The core competencies that we are trying to build and reinforce to deliver this strategy are:

- customer intimacy across channels and services;
- brand management, integrated marketing and a very detailed and evolving understanding of customer lifestyle needs;
- product and service innovation and integration;
- e-services and technology innovation/mastery/vision;
- integrated channel and operations management; and
- service efficiency and cost control.

In many of today's businesses it would be very hard to tick off more than a few of these as core competencies. The words may look easy, but the genuine competencies and the behavior they imply are hard to grow and require a degree of sustained attention.

The business gears its whole organization to drive change in the market and to stimulate new behavior and expectations in its customers.

Benefits of this strategy

This strategy is the most fun, the most dangerous and probably the most invigorating for staff. It is certainly the path which can equip the organization to prosper from even the most optimistic of forecasts of the development of e-commerce.

It does generate cost savings, but it needs a good deal of new money from somewhere, unless adjacent partners get together to co-fund the investments. This is happening more and more. Look at Time Warner and AOL, General Motors and Yahoo! and an increasing number of blue-chips who are sharing the equity on new ventures with innovative partners. Certain partners in manufacturing exchanges, like Transora, could become another example, given the ease with which the consumer-goods players have been able to raise £200m from members in two months. These organizations will suffer lots of divorces – but some will certainly hit pay-dirt.

I would summarize the benefits and disadvantages of this strategy as follows.

Benefits
- The benefits of previous scenarios.
- Substantial profit opportunities.
- Focuses energy and resources on the new competitive skills and markets.
- Creates a highly flexible business model.
- Increases the potential of becoming a long-term international branded player – hence achieving dominance.

Disadvantages
- High stretch for the organization.
- Higher investment path and risk.
- For the wrong company it would be a bridge too far.
- Requires an intelligent Darwinian culture and some good fortune.
- Bets the business to a serious degree.

Chase, Citi and Merrill Lynch look like being among the key financial-services players who will dominate personal finance across the channels. They are all going way beyond the simple financial planning offers; to create a revolutionary set of personalized financial-service infrastructures. On top of this they will add online shopping (ShopNow and Citiplaza) and a range of lifestyle portals and loyalty offers. These guys are obviously some of the 600-pound gorillas to watch out for. I feel sorry for sleepy retail banks and general insurance players, who are relying upon consumer inertia and blind loyalty to retain profitability and market share.

So, how do you develop a strategy which is appropriate for your business?

So, let's say you agree that you must now choose your strategy to survive the m-bomb and to prosper in these new markets. How do you establish which of these paths is broadly the right one for you? Then how do you decide what precisely you should be doing to make it happen, without betting the farm?

If you don't have a business strategy that embraces e-commerce and new channel opportunities then here is what I would suggest you do:

- Put a team together who can look at the opportunities and put practical strategy options together. Get some external help to stretch but also earth the thinking.
- Engage the top team in dissecting the alternatives and settling upon the path which fits the organization and the market.
- Align the investment budget, project portfolio and operating plans to chop out inefficiencies and drive in the new propositions and infrastructures. Set priorities and agree an investment approach to ensure the organization can deliver the vision, without too much fresh investment.

The approach that I will now go into in a bit more detail would typically take about three months in a large business. I have never known it to fail to energize the business and awaken the sleeping giant.

1   Brief an enthusiastic and experienced cross-functional team to brainstorm the pros and cons of these types of multi-channel scenarios, and their implications in your business. They should bring the alternative options to life, and produce tangible examples of how the services would develop. If they can't relate their thinking to practical products and services then either they aren't the right people, or you need help, or you should just go for "create the platform" and get some cost out.

It will save a huge amount of time if the teams start with the generic strategies that we detailed earlier. The board can then have a set of basic alternatives which they can debate. The options will have varying levels of ambition and various underlying implications in terms of investments, risks, benefits and competencies. In many cases a brief education process is needed here also – so the team and their colleagues really understand what is happening out there.

A great example of how ideas can flow comes from the brewing industry. If you are used to supplying beers and soft drinks to consumers, via a bunch of retail stores, there is now a logical journey you can go on: you can now assume that home delivery costs the same as via a high-street retailer and that you have a service agent going past every home twice per day.

- The team will first look at how to ensure their beer is well represented in all the new online channels which are emerging – exactly as they would in traditional retail channels. Just as you choose whether Krogers or Kmart is a high priority for trade-marketing investment and gaining shelf position for your products – so it is for the online channels. You need also to look positively at which online retailers and general services you need your products to be represented with (e.g. Webvan or Anew!)

- A party service or special event service is a very obvious first offer. The Internet can readily help you to pull together party ideas, recipes, online ordering of barbecue packages for ten guests – food, wine, beer, charcoal etc. Clearly one can go wild and put in masses of online content – but the burning question is whether the brand you create will be heard above the market noise and can get more than five orders a week.

  Most services like this are a great idea, but usually fail to attract sufficient share-of-mind in the key target groups. That is unless you can drive customers to the service using your pubs or bars.

  The new twist to making online sites work is to signpost them from the traditional retail world. If the team went for this type of service, they would think from a consumer viewpoint of how to scope a party/events service and which partners they would need. No one in their right mind just offers their own products on a lifestyle service like this! They need other company's products and services for it to make sense in the eyes of the customer.

- At the more extreme end of the spectrum the team can consider a potential revolution, which the young graduates used to dream about in workshops twenty years ago.

The ultimate here is the beer tap in the home – which sits next to the hot and cold water tap in the kitchen. The milk delivery man or home service agent can replace the small keg on the back wall whenever it is empty – and have the pump serviced from time to time. This used to be an April fool joke – "Heineken have just introduced beer taps into every home in Amsterdam". It is now actually affordable for very high-consumption households. The team should consider all the creative options and will evaluate and discuss the more advanced options which these new infrastructures make possible. They may end up rejecting these more ambitious options – but with people like EMI downloading music straight to the home it is silly not to think the unthinkable.

The best of the new e-fulfillment services are now able to touch each household twice per day at very low cost. The team can now seriously consider how to put much larger pack sizes into this channel – many of which were only suitable for cash and carry or entertainment centers and restaurants. Now that consumers don't have to pick the product off the shelf and carry it on the bus, a far more cost-effective and environmentally friendly option is available.

2   A well organized away-day should then be put together for the executive team to discuss the way forward. They typically work as follows:

- The CEO is invited to frame the challenge and set the tone of what they want to achieve.
- Someone with experience of the outside market and other sectors shows examples of what is going on out there, and gets the executives onto a level playing field of knowledge.
- The strawman strategies which the team have created are presented and pros and cons are drawn out. An open "Jerry Springer" style of debate is essential to flushing out the hard choices and gambles you could take. It should be a lot of fun if you organize it properly.
- The ideas and actions that come out of these discussions usually define the way forward. The cross-functional team can then be given a few more weeks to dig some more and frame a draft

strategy – ready for a rematch with the board and the start of the detailed planning activity (milestones, quick wins, longer-term goals, financial targets etc).

With the right support and approach we have found that even the most complex international business can carve out a powerful and well-conceived multi-channel strategy in two months.

In the current climate of change in the market I like to see this type of iterative process happening every year or so. However the most important step is to develop this first breakthrough view of which path to take to remodel the business.

If you are getting bored or are losing the will to live I would jump to Chapter 6. Otherwise do hang in there.

Walking the talk and living the strategy – aligning the project portfolio

The new strategy will only live if it causes some of the current "off-strategy" projects or investments to stop or be modified. Very few businesses will want to fund the new initiatives and infrastructures from new money alone. I have typically found in the past that between 15 and 20% of the project budget in a large business is being wasted. This is a lot of money. Part of this waste is caused by "hobby" projects, which appear vaguely enticing but which really achieve little. Waste can also be caused through basic inefficiency, when new operations or channel infrastructures are constantly being reinvented via one-off projects or poorly conceived initiatives. In one particular business we found over 400 separate operational projects, with a substantial level of duplication caused by people being unable to trust their colleagues to deliver anything for them (if I wait for you to deliver your bit of this I will grow old and die – so I will include everything I need in my initiative …).

Each complex business has its own cocktail of smart and oddly shaped projects. The following categorization of projects is one that I have found useful to help rationalize and negotiate a better portfolio. It is essential to balancing the demands of projects that are currently resourced, as well as those that are challenging to enter the portfolio:

- *The walking dead* – projects that are never quite starved of resources or put out of their misery. These poor old things stagger along, consuming small but useful amounts of scarce resources. Such projects which are slightly under-resourced and are ill conceived will often never finish. It takes a bold and decisive team to agree that resources must be focused on the priority initiatives, not spread like margarine. Put the walking dead out of their misery please!

- *The ugly sisters* – in a large company several projects will typically be building their own competitive versions of customer databases, call-center operations, online transaction services or administrative operations. You can often save a lot of money and time by crashing them together. Clearly, a mindless bureaucrat or the thought-police can also misuse this principle. It can be used as an excuse to stifle all innovation and create a series of plodding infrastructure mega-projects. If done properly however, the responsibility to build a shared service or component for the multi-channel business should be allocated to one lead project, and made to serve the other lead projects. The building of a flexible customer hub is a good example of this. In the fast-moving multi-channel world that is now emerging you cannot afford to let cynicism about creating dependencies and the expectation of mediocrity cause you to create incompatible and wasteful services. The ugly sisters are allowed to drain the heart of too many otherwise ambitious portfolios, which could produce breathtaking results if co-ordinated better.

- *Painting the wrong fences* – scarce internal resources should be used to drive step-changes in product and service innovation and to create substantial cost savings. You should outsource the many non-differentiating back-office and infrastructure activities. If you don't, you need to constantly invest in technology upgrades and regulatory changes to keep these "commodity" operations up to scratch. Every fence of this type that you own needs to be painted every three to five years. If you want to own all your own fences then ultimately you spend your whole life painting old fences, rather than building new houses which generate new sources of revenue.

To get the right balance of project investment you should task an aggressive team to use the following resource allocation model:

- Focus internal investment on differentiating competencies, which are key to delivering your strategy.
- Find specialist partners (they paint the fences that you can't afford to).
- Proactively manage the balance of customer and top-line impact versus cost saving (companies like Halifax and Unilever have great approaches and tools to do this – a subject for another day).
- Redesign and cut down the larger projects to use common components, which support the customer operating model we discussed earlier.
- Give the projects and initiatives which support the core of the strategy a clear priority (see initiatives outlined earlier in this chapter). Be prepared to stop other initiatives to divert resources.
- You must organize a bloodbath every quarter with all the stakeholders, to check and rebalance the portfolio as the multi-channel strategy unfolds.

I call it a bloodbath because it must hurt to be working. You will always have more demand for resources than you can possibly meet. Unless you are arguing and making tough choices you will fail. Spreading resource inadequately across too many projects will not work in these markets. Six months is a long time for a project to deliver. Two years is a complete joke.

I have used this approach successfully in many businesses – it maintains a great focus on things that matter and can save a fortune. It will also help to transform your speed to market.

The design for the customer operating model which we discussed earlier will allow you to shape the separate initiatives, so that they "plug and play" well in the eyes of the customer.

A well-briefed team can realign a complete portfolio within three months. They can often find the efficiency savings to fund the bulk of the new channel developments. The principles highlighted above provide a great framework for developing a strawman portfolio, which the board can adapt and confirm (using Genghis Khan as facilitator to keep everyone focused and honest). (See Fig. 5.4.)

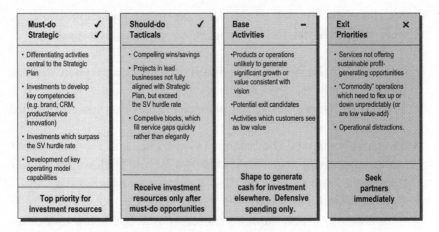

Must-do ✓ Strategic ✓	Should-do ✓ Tacticals	Base − Activities	Exit ✗ Priorities
• Differentiating activities central to the Strategic Plan • Investments to develop key competencies (e.g. brand, CRM, product/service innovation) • Investments which surpass the SV hurdle rate • Development of key operating model capabilities	• Compelling wins/savings • Projects in lead businesses not fully aligned with Strategic Plan, but exceed the SV hurdle rate • Competive blocks, which fill service gaps quickly rather than elegantly	•Products or operations unlikely to generate significant growth or value consistent with vision •Potential exit candidates •Activities which customers see as low value	• Services not offering sustainable profit-generating opportunities • "Commodity" operations which need to flex up or down unpredictably (or are low value-add) • Operational distractions.
Top priority for investment resources	Receive investment resources only after must-do opportunities	Shape to generate cash for investment elsewhere. Defensive spending only.	Seek partners immediately

Fig. 5.4   Principles of resource allocation and outsourcing.

This approach does not get done in five minutes, but I will briefly summarize how it would work for a global manufacturing business. You would typically have 150 serious projects going on around the world, with many costing over $1m – some a lot more. The team ruthlessly decide which functions or processes are exit or base priorities and stops any serious investments in these areas. You should find the operations in a lead territory which have a specific cost or service problem to solve, and get them to pull in a regional partner who has the skills to take over the exit priorities – be it for a call-center, logistics or table-stakes manufacturing. Exit priorities aren't just "commodity" operations like running your own employee benefits systems (why would you still be doing that?). They include the service and brand tail which will never survive in the m-world. If the team can't agree any exit priorities then change the team.

The trick with activities you agree as "must-do strategic" or "should-do tacticals" is to check you aren't addressing the same problem with five similar projects in different divisions or countries. You still want to do the tactical stuff if it carries a big payback – but if it doesn't you must not get sentimental. Chop it out. You need all the cash you can spare to build your multi-channel platforms, reposition your brand in many subtle ways and invest in getting the right strategic partnerships in place. Focus, focus and a bit of entrepreneurial pragmatism.

The right strategy and business design, translated into the right projects, which build the right competencies and capabilities. This will ensure that you go from acetate to action.

Many competitors will be stuck in acetate mode, which they will have paid $1m to some consultants to do for them. *Man cannot live by acetate alone.* Take advantage of their inertia to ensure that you aim, fire and reload while they are still procrastinating.

Summarizing the strategy to be the first brand standing

So you can now aim to be the first major brand in your sector to wake up to the m-bomb, and to march into the new market space which is only occupied by the entrepreneurs and the lightweights. A few dotcoms may have tilted gently at some of the broader lifestyle propositions and service offers, but most of them lack the depth and traditional skills to plant their flags permanently on the new turf. They are probably also very cheap to buy now. This is a good shortcut.

It is clear to see how Chase, Barnes & Noble, Gap, Sony and Walmart aim to be the first traditional brand standing in their sectors.

To be in the right shape you need to first decide whether your business is strong enough to go for an offensive or defensive set of priorities. The baseline defensive and cost-saving profile you should look at immediately is the "create the platform" strategy. This path helps you defend your existing customer base against predators – by progressively improving the way you touch and service the various sets of customers (hubbing your operations around the customers). You must set out to restructure your operations and increasingly focus what you do in-house on the new competitive areas. You will then get costs out and position yourself to be a lot more flexible in the market.

You should appoint a forward-looking group of managers to help your executive team to consider the more aggressive paths – either by moving faster to improve the proposition to create new profit streams or to actively drive the market to adopt a much broader offer, such as multi-shopping (high street and home, for bulk shop and convenience top-up …) and new household planning packages. The team should keep their feet on the ground, and must use research to validate the level of stretch and the opportunities for value generation.

The strategy that you adopt will dictate the partners you must rapidly acquire, the way you must realign your investment portfolio and the overall vision and commercial targets that you then communicate across your organization. The key is to openly and objectively look at the landscape in your markets as the m-bomb starts to hit. It is your judgement how aggressively and ambitious you will be. In all scenarios you will be on the front foot in using e-services and new partnerships to get costs out, and transform how you provide choices and services to customers.

If you have any doubts of how bold to be, I would suggest that you go for the cost-saving programs and build the platform to defend your turf. In fact, many companies like Procter & Gamble, Unilever and CGU prefer to use spinoffs or investment plays like ivillage and myhome to learn about the bolder "change the market" options, and to be ready to capture the competitive opportunities. They often choose to go cautiously with their traditional organizations.

Such a cautious approach is a risky business in my view, but it gets the antennae out there. It may work, as long as your big hairy competitors aren't quietly going much faster.

Beware – the ticking noise is growing louder.

Chapter 6

The Good, the Bad

and the Ugly

The multi-channel market is already out there – it just may not have appeared in your sales figures yet.

If you decide to sail to the new world it makes sense to observe or talk to those who have already made the journey before you. In this chapter we look at the way that smarter businesses who can't afford to waste time and money ensure that they learn from the experience of others. We will touch on how you analyze and pick out the areas of invention which are worth following and copying; how you then build your composite picture of a great business which will personify your chosen strategy. We will then touch on how you save millions of dollars, and a year or two, to shortcut the mistakes of others.

I believe more strongly than ever now that anyone who reinvents their new customer offerings and Internet operations from scratch is a fool. There are many businesses out there that are trying to weld the old and the new together in various smart ways.

The bones of the ideal solution and service design for your business are already out there – evolved, working and proven. They may not be there in your sector or territory, but given the convergence of business models enabled by the Internet (and the sheer breadth of recent experimentation), I doubt that yours will be the first footprints on the beach. You just need to recognize the pieces that are important for you, and weave them together in your own special way to beat the pants off the competition. You need to know where to look and then analyze and interpret what makes the early adopters successful. By doing this you can follow their lead and reduce your risks dramatically.

In the Webb Partnership (www.thewebbpartnership.com) we first started to pick out the good, the bad and the ugly three years ago, because we had to build breakthrough operations which linked the old and the new channels from scratch – and there was no rulebook. When you first touch a new world and you don't understand how to survive, the first rule is to observe and then learn from the things around you – very quickly. See what grows well and easily and, by their absence, what probably dies and is not worth planting. See what the animals or natives choose to eat and what they avoid – they will have learnt some lessons that are probably important for you.

Lessons from 1000 years of new channel innovation

The Internet and the new "lifestyle" or bundled services have not been out there for many years, but take the experience of hundreds of innovative companies over a few years and it is still entirely possible to find and analyze "1000 years of experience" and use it to your advantage. You just need to look across countries and sectors, as we started to do several years back. Fairly soon we will get to ten thousand company years of experience from which our best practice can draw upon even more reliably. So this is not about clever theories and naïve projections – it is about finding who else has gone where you are headed and using them as your reference point. This approach collapses time and risk dramatically.

So how does it work in the context of building a successful multi-channel business?

First we categorized the learning we needed to gain about this new world, so that we could understand success and failure intelligently. We geared our analysis to help us to build successful operational services which were compelling and made money – rather than for any arid intellectual purpose.

We sought out good, bad and ugly examples of:

1 *Clicks and bricks or new-economy services which make money!*
   Any old fool can use the Web as a discount channel and buy market share. When you look back at the first three years there were many

such fools – and many have lost their innocence now. You still have to look hard to find the profitable ones though.

2   *Services which are truly intimate and offer customers a closer relationship.* Good Websites and relationship services are designed to remember what customers tell them and offer tailored services, reward customer loyalty, etc. They should display the symptoms of an operational customer hub, but also a clear understanding of how to build and foster advanced relationships.

3   *Innovative new services or propositions which change the rules.* Bad examples are often just a catalog which has been crudely translated to the Internet, or the same old service offered lamely in the new channel. The good guys use the new medium to offer things that just weren't possible before – e.g. online grocery shopping with the ability to automatically block high-fat products or items containing nuts. Imagine how such a simple service can offer a great lifestyle benefit for a family with a nut allergy or a health conscious family. You could never do this in a traditional store. Only the power of the PC and the Internet can sort and present products individually for up to 100 million different consumers.

4   *Friendly and highly intuitive services, rather than complex or self-important services which don't get the job done easily.* Well-designed online and call-center operations should help you to complete your chosen transaction in seconds, with options to do other useful, but secondary things placed at your disposal but not in your face. Like inside an airplane cockpit, the key instruments are in line of sight and the tools to take off, land and navigate are never out of reach. We find it incredibly easy to unearth hundreds of really pathetic online services. It looks like the chairman's son has designed a clever service but didn't bother to think about the customer's priorities and how their minds would work. The arrogance and complacency of many businesses is breathtaking, and you often see it in sharp relief in their Websites or when using their deeply irritating services by phone.

5   *Great extensions of the brand in the new channels.* These new dialog and servicing channels are really just a new route to the customer. They should still breathe the brand values that you see in a physical store, in TV advertising and in traditional product packag-

ing. This cross-channel feel and branding is where companies like Guinness excel. Conversely the brand managers who stand by and allow some of the services that we see launched on an unsuspecting world should be shot. Better to do nothing than to launch an ugly or brash service which prostitutes your brand image.

6   *Seamless and integrated customer experiences across the channels.* A good example here is that some Internet services offer a "call me" button – in case you get lost online and want to speak to a human being. The person you talk to at the call-center should also see the Internet order you were halfway through and can finish it for you. They also see all your personal customer hub information, so can treat you in the way that is most appropriate. Others like Lands End could let you shop with a friend online, just as you would expect to do in Donna Karen.

From a different angle, it is obvious in some services that when you complete the transaction the job is done now – one touch was all it took to set up, activate, launch back-office processes and set any special follow-up in motion. Conversely the bad services will tell you enormous amounts about their products and services, but you can't order them (as frustrating as coitus interruptus). Or they will transparently be creating the equivalent of an e-mail, which you can tell will create error-prone manual processes in a day or so when they try to do what you wanted – what a criminal waste of opportunity and money.

We have found it useful to analyze what we see in the market in many other ways as well, based on the needs of specific markets, but this core set is a must for everyone who is looking to get the basics right.

Choosing your reference companies

So who are some examples of the good, bad and the ugly that we should be using as reference points today?

Clearly I could bore you to death with lists of companies from the thousands that we have evaluated or continue to track today who are bad and ugly. Rather than do that (and risk all the potential litigation) I will offer a few carefully chosen examples, which I can safely do here.

I love Heinz's proposition for expatriates who want to ensure that their babies stay healthy whilst they are far from home. Not risking your baby's health in a strange land is a good example of a strong customer need! There are many more reasons why this service is an act of genius. The Internet ordering channel fits perfectly with the target expatriate segment, who already mostly use e-mail and the Web to stay in touch. The target customers will happily pay full retail price and shipping for such a useful service, which meets their emotional as well as rational needs. The delivery model is great, given that people can plan ahead and international parcel delivery is ideal for the volume and value involved. There is no pioneering infrastructure needed. The service avoids channel conflict with food retailers in the home market. Heinz never sell US products to Americans living in the US, so Walmart are happy. And at the same time they learn more about home shopping and online marketing. What a brilliant execution – I wonder it if was partly luck or a really smart team in Heinz. If you were in the team who dreamt this one up please call me and I will buy you a lazy lunch at a hostelry of your choice.

I still will never quote Amazon as an example for anyone to follow on making money or building great multi-channel operations or supply chain – but the way they personalize is a good example of how intimacy can and should evolve. Try ordering a book a month from them and see how they develop the relationship, as well as your ability to tailor your navigation. Many lead businesses use the Netperceptions personalization engine to very good effect – it is best of breed and I would recommend it to you. I also find that Musicmaker's personalized CDs and Kickers personalized shoes (designed to your online spec. and made and shipped in 15 days) show how the unimaginative manufacturers may be easily outflanked.

On the other hand – I wonder why Easyjet, on their early car rental site, immediately seemed to forget everything that they must already know about you from the existing relationship, and repeatedly asked for my address details which I found onerous and irritating.

On the subject of avoiding conflict with existing distribution channels, I find Procter & Gamble's approach with cosmetics compelling. As we mentioned earlier, Reflect.com (www.reflect.com)

is a service they co-own, offering a personalized range of products, which they can honestly tell the retailers are different from the normal consumer units – hence not a direct threat. At this moment they are getting away with selling directly to consumers and Walmart or Macey's are not killing them for it – good for them. It is also interesting that they have done this with a joint venture, and different manufacturing assets and approach to the ones they use in their core business. Like many successful traditional businesses they resort to using new business models and new brands to pioneer the new channels.

This is sad in some ways, given the investment in existing brands and the fact that a blue-chip organization really ought to be able to make the existing elephant dance. This is a test you should apply for your business. Does your organization have the flexibility and imagination to do this on your own – or do you need to enter the three legged race with a latter day Carl Lewis? It is good if your company culture can reinvent itself to build upon your existing brand and the back-office and supply-chain processes that you already have. If not though it is good to quickly admit defeat and get on with building the future with a separate set of brands and organization. Either route is far better than falling between the two stools and doing nothing of substance at speed. If you are a company who can do it with your traditional brand then you get a holiday for three in the Caribbean. The future will definitely be yours.

Tesco in the UK are a great example of a company who are leveraging their existing retail brand into home shopping and new product areas. They have followed their highly successful service to the home, for traditional grocery products, with a new set of non-grocery products which will gradually eat away at the banks, book and music retailers and other consumer services. They are also a world leader in pioneering new consumer access devices, such as the innovative scan technologies from specialists such as Symbol (which show that the mass market is not just about PCs). Tesco's brand is translating well to the direct channels, whereas I look at people like Mondi and Ralph Lauren and wonder why they left their online brand presence so subterranean for so long (type Ralph Lauren into any search engine and see how the brand feels. Is anyone at home? Have they fixed it yet?)

Sobering examples from across the channels

Turning to the sleepy travel business, I have been astonished at how British Airways throw their schedules in your face, rather than helping you more systematically to get from Chicago to London when you want to go (and if a BA flight is suitable, then great). They should look at the consumer need slightly ahead of the crude product push. BA is now getting together with other airlines to use infrastructure across Europe based on GetThere, so it may help solve this problem for them. On a slightly brighter note you can check KLM and see how they have a useful link to a human being at a call-center, showing how the multi-channel game can be presented in a nice way.

> Going back to BA, they also have serious channel problems in my view. I know from bitter experience that they can have the most appalling way of penalizing the customer for their own inability to control their channels. A little while ago I booked a flight from London to New York via a travel agent in Hamburg, because it was substantially cheaper than buying it in London. That is a serious issue in itself – cross subsidization is usually a sign of a deeper malaise. When I got on the Hamburg–New York flight in London, a BA person then grilled me very publicly in the executive lounge about whether I really boarded a connecting flight in Hamburg before I started the London–New York leg. As I could not prove that I was on the original Hamburg flight they then proceeded to cancel my ticket and make it as tedious and as humiliating as they possibly could. I can perhaps generalize a message here. Making a customer suffer for what appears to be your own incompetence in controlling your sales channels and your prices is unforgivable in my book. God help a business who behaves that way. From spending a fortune with them over the years, from Jakarta to Santiago, I will now only fly BA if they are the only carrier on a route. From advocate to poisonous detractor in one short year. Don't put your customers in difficult situations because of your inability to solve your channel problems – they will never forgive you.

To get away from ugly things you may want to check out a new travel experience with GetThere, (www.getthere.com). They do a wonderful job of extending your simple travel request (as a service primarily to businesses) with intuitive and simple ways to get the job done and to give city details, hotels etc. Everything is just a few clicks away and they get the basics right – such as automatically knowing that the pick list for a return flight should start after the date of the outbound journey. This sounds a blindingly obvious design feature, but check yourself how many novices are building online services which are too lazy to program simple but important details like that. Unbelievable.

The power of imagination, innovation and imitation

I could go on forever like this, but the point of course is not related to these specific examples as we look at them at this moment in time. The good and bad examples change month by month. The point of these analyses lie in the following principles:

1   Don't build a service as if you were Livingstone, discovering Africa for the first time. Get a life and learn from all the others. The reference points for this moment in time for a consumer goods retailer might be to build a service with:
    • the searching power and function of Britannica
    • the personalization of Musicmaker or Amazon
    • the ease of use of GetThere
    • the range and online performance of Tesco
    • the multi-channel services of Merita Bank, Landsend, KLM or Fedex
    • the imagination of Heinz or P&G
    • the branding of GAP or Guinness
    On thewebbpartnership.com you can find the latest equivalent of this reference list (another great example of realtime multi-channel services).
        Every modern and progressive business should keep their finger on the good, bad and ugly pulse of multi-channel operations. Research them yourself continuously or get some help. But for heaven's sake take a few weeks to interpret these composite

design principles, propositions and relationships that have evolved successfully in the market.

2   Decide proactively whether you want to do a Home-Depot (reportedly telling Black & Decker in the US that if they go direct they will be in trouble) or a Best-Buy (acknowledging that HP will sell direct also – treating it as healthy competition, but feeling confident that they should be able to provide a range and service edge). I know whose approach I prefer. If you are a manufacturer, decide if your channel strategy is more like Heinz or P&G or like Mars or Nestlé (who seem to have more cautious "toe in the water" approaches). There are many confidential stories that I cannot tell, but I would usually advise larger businesses to find a bold route through the bushes, rather than stick your head in a bucket.

3   Don't forget that your competitor-monitoring activity now needs to focus across a range of sectors – Walmart, Microsoft or GAP could eat your next lunch just as easily as yesterday's competitor. Just look at your P&L collapse when half of your most profitable and promiscuous customers get enticed elsewhere in the next three years. Similarly you must worry about the new competitor, who is sharing marketing and back-office costs across twice your potential market geography and all the potential mass-market channels (while you are just hitting the high street).

4   There has never been a market like this one, with so much at stake and such a Darwinian process under way. Use your own particular filter and view of the good, the bad and the ugly to educate your

---

I only found out a few years ago that Charles Dickens used to publish his books a chapter at a time. This is why many chapters end with a little bit of tension and "watch this space – what happens next?" In those days it was a sound economic model for delivering fiction to the masses. We now have Frederick Forsyth serialising his book Quintet exclusively on the Internet – by instalments. You should not routinely have to go back 100 years for innovative ideas, but do at least look around you at parallel sectors and markets to stimulate your thinking.

people, benchmark your offerings and challenge your business and cost model. If you keep digging the same old ditch you will certainly fall victim to the m-bomb. You will also inevitably fall victim sometime in the next five years to a combination of a predator and a worried set of shareholders.

Imagination is good, innovation is vital, but the ability to interpret and emulate success is everything.

Part 3

Riding the Multi-channel Tiger

So you now have a good view of your strategy which will take the business forward. You have scanned the best initiatives around to give you a range of implementation ideas and reference points.

You will hopefully have carried out at least some customer research, which tells you how far you can stretch your existing brand and which types of customer will respond to the different services that you could readily develop.

The biggest challenge remains to take the potential of a well-designed customer operating model and a set of innovative services and to then actually go and make money with them, building upon what you have inherited in your traditional business. You are probably not starting with a blank slate – you have a big organization, many smart people and a network of offices, processing centres, factories, warehouses, brand teams and IT infrastructures.

You now also have a range of new capabilities to build and new partners to get into bed with, depending upon the type of strategy you adopt.

In this section of the book we will again draw from a great deal of early experience, to look at how you should go about achieving this transition to a multi-channel business effectively without forgetting that your customers have to see a powerful difference in your services within the first six months. We will also look at how you will need to change your organization, so that you can make money and achieve the right level of agility.

Chapter 7

Implementing the Multi-channel Business (and Getting to Market Quickly with the Right Services)

We will first look at the secrets of turning a good multi-channel vision and strategy into a credible plan that everyone understands.

Figure 7.1 illustrates the tools and approach that we will now go into in more detail.

You will notice that I am still a fan of the good old-fashioned disciplines of annual operating plans (contracts) for business units,

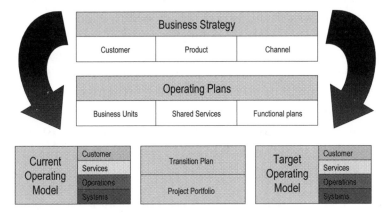

Fig. 7.1 Developing the operating model and transition plan.

functions and shared services. The tried and tested value of agreeing milestones, economic payback, market-share targets and portfolio management still hold as true as ever in this new world.

The model shown above ties the strategy, which we selected for the business in Chapter 5, to a set of firm operating plans which managers can execute. In a modern business the overall strategy needs to be reflected in a coherent set of customer, product and channel strategies. Kodak know that the product strategy and underlying research plans must be shaped and balanced, so that scarce dollars are working towards the right set of propositions. These propositions must work well with the range of delivery channels that the business is attacking – detailed in the channel or "go to market" strategy. The customer strategy speaks for itself – and is a driving force that anchors the priorities elsewhere and which provides the rationale for the overall performance growth of the business.

These strategies must be developed carefully, and in the light of the market forces and eruptions that we have discussed. They must be translated into operating plans to walk the talk and to guide the business day-to-day. Without these, the troops won't march in unison and will only have a fluffy idea of where the anthill needs to move to. Underpinning these adjustments in priorities and plans is the transition plan and the implementation activity – which we will discuss more now. The base of the diagram highlights how you must chart your course and agree your speed of change: from how you serve customers and operate today (current operating model), to how your multi-channel strategy dictates that you need to operate in order to survive and prosper in the future (target operating model).

The operating models are defined in terms of customer, services, operations and systems, along the lines that we talked about in Chapter 4 (using the m-maps as a key tool). This forces the operations to align to customer needs and channel opportunities.

This light but highly choreographed structure allows the board to manage the change. It unleashes the management to reinvent and extend the operations, in line with the chosen strategy and the commercial realities.

Any bright young thing who says "just trust me" and rejects all plans and measures is as big and as dangerous an idiot as the young and old fogies who resist the need for change. Shareholders, management and staff need their levers and contracts, but they must be reframed to move the business faster than almost anyone is used to, so that the multi-channel business is created without delay.

So how do you get the elephant to dance, without forgetting to keep collecting the money from the traditional popcorn stands and the sale of balloons?

The core of it is to create an aggressive transition plan, which steps the business forward in an ambitious but manageable way. *The plan should aim to migrate internal processes and customer services from the current muddle and mess to a far more customer-centric and efficient multi-channel mess.*

The transition plan to an m-business

It is fairly obvious from what we see out there that you cannot eat this particular wedding cake in one go. The smart companies elect to fund a lot of the investment required for the new services from a combination of new cost-saving initiatives and increased reliance upon well chosen partnerships. The broad strategy you have chosen must now be translated into a prioritized, achievable and well-resourced transition plan.

The purpose of a good change plan is to:

- Set the broad direction and pace of organizational change and resource deployment.
- Plot the best path from the current balance of operations to the target operating model and services.
- Define staged targets and assumptions.
- Project the costs and benefits.
- Assist alignment of existing and planned initiatives to a coherent set of infrastructures and customer outcomes.
- Indicate the needs for partners and focus the selection process.

The plan should earth your grand ideas.

The plan will soon reveal whether your overall strategy makes commercial sense. The plan must encompass all major functions and operations and can typically be put together by a strong internal team in two to three months. A bit of external salt and pepper is good, but I am very wary of organizations that employ a $4 million piece of consultancy to plan their future. A few board workshops along the way are of course essential, but the key is to get on with commissioning a lead team to define and align the main components of implementation to get you where you need to be. The companies who have wasted tens of millions on ill-considered initiatives, which customers have voted against, have usually avoided the pragmatic checkpoint and planning process which we will now go into more deeply.

First identify your starting point

To plan your evolution, from single-channel, simple proposition to multi-channel and bundled proposition, you need to quickly confirm and agree your going-in position (sounds obvious, doesn't it – but it will surprise you what you learn from this).

To help you to gauge where your business is on the transition curve, it is worth picking out where most traditional businesses are with their current operating model.

It will typically look something like this.

Customer-facing processes
You will probably find that you have:

- Primarily "one size fits all" services and products – all customers get roughly the same deal.
- No active customer relationship database is used to inform the way that you touch customers – a more retrospective analysis approach may be being used, but customers don't "feel it."
- Customer communication between the various channels is fairly uncoordinated (direct marketing, outbound telesales ...)
- There is a mix of workflow and manual processes across mail handling, call-center, inquiries/complaints, sales. You are a long way from "one multi-channel touch."
- Low function operations are becoming available for customers to serve themselves, but it is very slow in coming.

- Incompatible customer recognition and welcome processes are used across the channels (e.g. they need to remember different pass codes and pin numbers).

Ask your team how many of these you would tick off – be honest.

Internal processes
On the plus side, your internal activities are probably better placed. You may find:

- Back-office and sales administration processes are well automated and optimized (using an expensive monster like SAP…)
- Great functional approaches are in place for accounting, manufacturing, actuarial, treasury.
- Short-term product and materials call-off is advanced, but vendor owned replenishment and planning are in their infancy.
- Product innovation and R&D are optimized internally in stovepipes, but it is slow, expensive and mystical. On the other hand the marketing processes are fast, whilst still being expensive and mystical.

Profits are flowing fairly well. The bean-counters will typically be guarding the portfolio and may influence investment disproportionately. They have looked after the internal basics well, and the advertising and IT plans look relatively healthy in isolation. However the chances are that the competitors are not exactly quaking in their boots, particularly the international ones.

Your team will need to go into more detail of course, as they capture your going-in position. You can hopefully see how you can map your starting point from which you set sail for the m-world.

Themes to guide your plans

So how do you shape your plan "to build the platform" or beyond?

We are running a business here – not trying to win a mixed-economy glamour contest. The transition plan must factor in the following goals, alongside the evergreen themes of keeping the profit engines delivering.

The plan must:

- Deliver obvious e-business quick wins which cut costs and give the customers some early signs of innovation.
- Coincide with emerging customer needs for improved service and dialog.
- Provide clear competitive differentiators, which customers will recognize in the new market – not just traditional product-performance benefits which would be important in the single-channel market. If in doubt, you must at least offer more convenience and added value.
- Leverage customer information intelligently across channels and functions.
- Provide key customer segments with their access channel of choice, but recognize that customers are not equal and therefore some services, prices or offers are differentiated. This demands more than charging some customers to use branches of banks in the high street or only offering free delivery to big spenders.
- Help customers to serve themselves – like Staples, who have introduced friendly and powerful intranet-based ordering of office supplies. Or in corporate banking, where the customer is provided with the tools to manage their financial affairs directly, without expensive sales or account people involved in the day to day.
- Support new services robustly and scaleably. Avoid quick and dirty solutions based on cul-de-sac operations. Do it quickly, but use partners who can do it properly.
- Enable extension of the proposition to adjacent areas of customer need – you could find non-competitive partners whose services dovetail with yours. Seeing Marsh insurance brokers team up with Ford cars should show you the way here.
- Respond always to commercial realities (affordability, people constraints, value generation). You will look at value generation differently, but you are still running a commercial business.
- Reward loyalty for customers and partners in a meaningful way. In some cases you should be prepared to share equity with partners – as P&G have done with their individualized cosmetics operation.

You can see hopefully how these themes tie into the m-bomb market pressures that we covered in Part 1.

How your target operations may look

It is dangerous to generalize and pretend this is all strategy-by-numbers. But from working with hundreds of businesses one can define a typical target profile. Clearly the target operating model and multi-channel services will vary by business and sector, but a typical model that you must aim for will include the following.

Capabilities which customers will recognize

These features are clearly very desirable if you want to move the market:

- Tailored or mass-customized services, which offer different customer sets the products and relationships that meet their needs. One extreme example is the new luxury-goods businesses which will offer the seriously rich customers the services of a personal shopper, who will go and get products for them. These services are available in the big cities already.
- Different pricing and loyalty benefits, so that heartland and loyal customers get a better deal than others.
- Customer contact and servicing operates across channels, e.g. if I call you, then visit a store or come in online, your people know about my issues and needs.
- Co-ordinated communication and sales – if you offer me a loan via the post then I know that you won't make the same offer two days later when I ring the call center.
- One-touch processes for the most important customer interactions – if you come in online, or phone in to place an order or change your address, it happens automatically and immediately.
- Self-service/execution for customers is an attractive option – I can do it all myself via the Web if I choose.

- Personal agents or service brokers are "plugging & playing" on behalf of customers. Amazon's personalized recommendations of books you should like is a simple example. Companies like Hewlett-Packard and NetPerceptions have great technologies which make the Web work for you, rather than make you work the Web. Personal agents can of course be people who have the tools to serve you well. In the future though they will increasingly be smart technology – navigating the channels and the Web on your behalf.

Internal capabilities which make you agile and cost efficient

The following features are vital to service delivery and funding the future. Choose what is important to your business.

- You have a one-touch electronic supply-chain layer – so that all partners and specialist systems that move or plan stock are intercepting your intranet stock monitor – streamlining stock and using track and trace to pick up and respond to problems on the hoof.
- Inventory and quality responsibilities are delegated upstream – suppliers will automatically manage your materials availability and will operate within an advanced certification process.
- Auction or "make-to-bid" approaches are used selectively. For high-volume routes the shippers or manufacturers will bid via real-time Web services to fulfil your needs (many table-stakes things you used to do in house are now bought in).
- Soft product innovation processes are streamlined – your teams are using simple "funnel" processes to co-ordinate decision-making on projects at key delivery stages. They have introduced advanced teamworking approaches and antennae customers (representative customers that you have a close dialog with, so you can test new ideas) all as part of the rapid development process. This is a topic for a whole book in itself – so I won't try to oversimplify too much here.
- Product information and "catalog" processes are one-touch – sales staff, customers and agents all have the same Internet-based information support. The time taken to launch and support new

products is collapsed to a fraction of what you used to think of as normal.

- Your product operations remain stovepiped (in-house or via third parties), but they are smartly bundled so that customers see a high perceived rate of innovation (the wonders of a product hub).
- Your internal energies and headcount are focused on the capabilities which really matter – brand, innovation, managing customer relationships and end-to-end service management.

Each of these capabilities can be introduced and harnessed to extract hard benefits in even the most complex business, in six to nine months. The trick is to use proven approaches, business designs and technologies which have been developed from the experience of others.

No business can afford to develop them all in parallel, and no one has the management cover to drive everything at once. For this reason you need to set your priorities and decide your implementation phasing. Please don't be arrogant about this – learn shamelessly from the experience of others.

Your challenge now is to plan the transition to this type of business. A transition plan may look like the "averaged" example in Fig. 7.2, which is in line with the type of plan that the best businesses in the world are going after.

The priority in businesses I respect most is to introduce customer-facing benefits and cost savings very early, but to plan substantial changes to services and the overall value chain for the medium term. This is where businesses like Walmart, Reuters and Tesco have scored well.

You can see that the typical example we have shown in Fig. 7.2 has the new customer offerings and the quick wins as the initial priority – quite right too.

You must establish hard commercial targets for 9, 18 and 36 months, or your team may lose their way. It is very easy for transition teams to get excited about the architectures and glossy propositions. They can easily forget about the need to make the numbers (nothing changes really).

Clearly your team will shape the phases and the milestones based on what makes the most sense in your market. I would suggest though

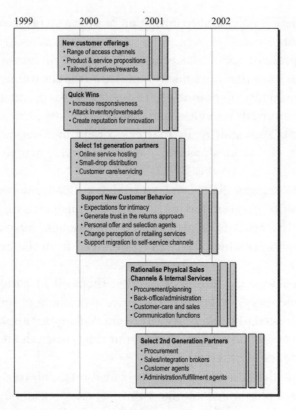

Fig. 7.2 Overview of a typical transition plan.

Key measures at regular milestones:

- Number of new channel and multi-channel customers
- Cost-savings banked
- Innovation rate, as perceived by customers
- Share-of-voice and market in target online segments
- Perception of what the brand stands for
- Income from new profit streams

that you point them at this generic plan as a strawman, and ask them to produce a detailed version of their own for discussion with the board. If they are not confident that they can create the plan in a few months then swap them out. They should not drive down into

In the US over half of the new home grocery players have folded during 2000. No great surprises there, given the ludicrous economic models that most of them created, but why didn't they set firmer commercial milestones for their businesses? In some other territories the online grocery market is going ballistic – and is even in danger of becoming profitable. Strange but true.

the specific actions and costs until the broad phases of change and priorities are agreed. They should tie the shape of the plans to the strategy that has been developed, from the approaches we discussed in the earlier chapters.

The transition plan is where the senior teams match the level and type of action to the level of ambition in the strategy. A "change the market" plan will necessarily have a lot of stretch in it – as you can see from the transition plan shown earlier.

Bringing the transition plan to life – creating the snapshots

To further illustrate the shape of a typical change plan, I should give an example of an apparel business, which primarily operates currently using high street retail outlets and a select number of specialized catalog brands.

The transition plan can be translated into snapshots of what the business should look like in 9, 18 and 36 months.

Transition plan milestones and stages

End-state 1 (9 months)
- The first-stage customer relationship systems are in place. A mix of automatic and semi-manual interfaces are providing all channels with information on customer purchase history, sales propensity, contact history and risk profile for credit scoring.

- The "proof-of-concept" online/PC service is in trial with around 10,000 consumers. As a result of the consumer research and the operational learning from the proof-of-concept, the plans to develop the proposition and the service are now well advanced.
- A confident and aggressive integrated marketing campaign is now on the starting blocks, with a plan to deliver a controlled but continuous stream of service improvements. Whenever a customer phones in, a well-targeted sales offer can be made. Customers largely see this as positive and useful. This relationship process is also now feeding into keeping the propositions ahead of the game, e.g. modular garments coming shortly.
- Quality partners have been selected to support the specialist aspects of customer-care and fulfillment operations – slimming down the in-house operations.

End-state 2 (18 months)

- The customer relationship systems are now supporting highly personalized promotions, bundled-offers and mass-customized lifestyle offers in whichever channel the customer chooses to use (PC, phone, digital-TV, store visit, WAP phone etc.).
- The online services are available and well-supported at home, in workplaces via corporate intranets and via kiosks in high footfall locations in-store.
- The fully personalized modular garment service is on offer. The family clothing plan is in pilot – helping you to finance and provide your children's needs as they grow.
- European rollout of the direct service is complete, using the merchandising model from the US parent. Service delivery and fulfillment partners who could not meet the service level standards have been replaced.
- The upstream supply-chain relationships have now been transformed in the many areas where there is volatility of demand. The electronic supply-chain layer is now serving the "guaranteed" baseline for the more evergreen and seasonal ranges. More specialized demand for fashion items is supported, using vendor-managed replenishment processes via the Web. The most volatile and multi-source demand is using demand/bid processes on a real-time basis.

- The new channels have now got a permanent leadership structure and sales/profit management processes. In other words, a senior line manager will be dying in the ditch to build volume and profit for the online service and home channel, as a separate profit centre.

End-state 3 (36 months)
- Some high street outlets have now been sold off and new mobile "try-out" approaches for new clothing ranges established, using a variety of formats (in offices, mobile mall changing rooms, at home neighbourhood events etc.).
- Relationships with third-party customer-care, procurement brokers and personal-needs agents are likely to be well-established. Specific functions will have evolved to manage these channels and initial supply-chains, supporting both traditional channels as well as the new channels.

These end states are slightly over the top to protect the innocent, but hopefully they will illustrate the point. In your business it is important to develop a similar set of snapshots of how the business will operate to bring the changes to life – so that you can ensure that everyone in the business can understand just how the evolution of the business will impact their part of the operation. The milestones provide a very tangible set of measures for senior management.

Pausing to inject a little humility

So we have now distilled the experience from a wide range of market-leading elephants who are learning to samba, step by step, month by month.

By avoiding the "trust me" approach to multi-channel developments you will force the business to set out clear plans, which migrate the current single-channel mess to the multi-channel mess. By plotting the most pragmatic path from A to B you will get yourself into a position where you can use your traditional business judgement to reassure yourself:

- that we can afford it;
- that we believe these plans are viable and doable;
- that we have been able to translate what felt like a compelling strategy into a set of plans that our people buy into and understand; [This approach of translating the new vision into a practical set of plans works every time to test the grander ideas out. I have seen a number of businesses quietly step back from a "change the market strategy," once they have seen the hard implications and accept a more realistic vision.]
- that the prize is worth the risk to the current peaceful existence which we all kind of like;
- the excitable planners have left some of the sex and sizzle until later, with some quick tangible wins coming through early on; and
- that the perceived benefits to customers (and analysts) will be a key focus for our combined energies.

That is all good stuff, because it will introduce a high level of familiarity and certainty in an investment area which many business leaders have thought of as a black art.

A major problem still remains though. There is no way that you can sensibly research how your customers will react with their hearts and wallets to these new convenience channels and propositions. You can drag 15 customers into a focus group with a fine Chianti and some nice fava beans and talk to them about your planned services. The loud guy in the red check pants will foam at the mouth about the new ideas and will offer a half of his monthly spending to the company who offers him the time savings or the one-stop shopping. He will also produce a set of random views on how Calvin Klein should really front up the service, rather than you. He is really motivated by sport, sex and self-expression. A bit of a man thing perhaps. Guys like that tend to change the tone of debate and flush out a rainbow of opinions on what is important. You can get some ideas but can you really bet your business on it?

I organized a focus group a few months ago for an organic and health-food company, where we had a rather interesting mix of views coming through – but of all the people there, one woman influenced me most. She epitomized the forward-looking volume shopper, who was very willing to pay for services which met her needs. She was

I am continually astonished how our children and some of our weirder colleagues are all sending huge numbers of SMS messages to each other. "will meet u at park at 3"; "true u fancy Sheila?"; "report with u when u get to office." I have never met such a ridiculous consumer access device as the keypad of a tiny mobile phone. It breaks all the rules of ergonomics, and yet it does have the benefit of being ubiquitous, cheap (a few cents per message) and fashionable (not to be underestimated). I have been amazed that mobile messaging has gone ballistic in the way it has – but having seen the consumer habit come out of nowhere you need to learn how to work with it to your advantage.

desperate for convenience and healthy options for her family and would offer disproportionate loyalty to the brand which gave it to her.

The problem of course is that we really can only get signals of the likely response to more radical propositions from research, and we can't really trust it too heavily. The m-bomb involves significant changes to customer buying behavior. It involves the evolution of completely new supply chains which change the service model quite dramatically. If you use the good, bad and ugly lessons from the market, you can reduce the risks a lot – but the bolder you get, the more you will be flying by instinct. Those who developed the Sony Walkman, the MP3 player and the smart phone had to walk this path.

So be humble – and know that your strategy and transition plan must be tested in the heat of the market at every stage. You need a Darwinian approach to testing new offers in the market very quickly – and if they work you then scale the hell out of them.

Now let's see how the winners get this to work – using what we call the P·R·I·C·E Approach™.

Testing and extending the offer – the last component of strategy

The forces of darkness will gather quickly if the first manifestation of your online service or extended offer is not successful. This project and implementation approach, which we will now discuss, is a vital part of the customer understanding process – as you learn quickly how customers will respond to new cross-channel services and broader propositions. You must still use anecdotal evidence and qualitative research of what customers need as far as you can, but you must accept that many of the changes that you will drive in will be beyond the range of normal consumer testing.

Over recent years we have distilled and learnt how to bottle a relatively safe and guaranteed approach to achieving successful market entry with multi-channel offers in six months, without forgetting the broader goals of robustness and profitability. We call it the P·R·I·C·E Approach – Process and Rules for Implementing m-Commerce Effectively™.

It is a structured approach to a complex and unfamiliar process, which forces the business team to think through the objectives of the central "clicks and mortar" service or new proposition clearly, and then to ensure that a rounded offering is introduced quickly. In all cases the service must meet the strong operational criteria we have talked about earlier. The detail of the approach is not a topic for senior management – but at the high level is summarized in the following pages. This is probably a section that you may wish to come back to later or miss completely, so you may want to skip to page 130.

I would suggest that you ask your lead teams to follow this approach or use the checklist on the pages which follow.

Following the P·R·I·C·E Approach™

For each major initiative which is in your transition plan you must form a project team who can rapidly step through the following approach. These pragmatic steps are designed to make sure that the planning, operational approach and implementation are taken forward with the right ingredients for success.

Step 1: confirm the objectives of the new service

It is important to agree the precise benefits that are being targeted – for you, for your customers and for partners. These should be as specific as possible, so as to flush out confusions of purpose at the outset and to shape the solutions that will be developed. Benefits to be targeted could include specified service improvements or cost reductions, ease of ordering and communication, new product benefits or added value, increased channel choice, buzz, deepening of relationships with high-value customers or reaching new markets.

Get away from platitudes and hopeless ambition – what will be your measure of success for you and your customers?

Step 2: define your customer operating model

You must decide whether you want to build upon your main brand or whether you want to create a new brand and an entirely new proposition. For a traditional business it is usually better to open new access channels as a complement to your existing business model (offering preferred customers more choices and services), but the current business can be so slow and bureaucratic that it would kill the new channel at birth. Senior teams often think that they want radical new propositions, but their most important customers are really looking for simple cross-channel services and greater convenience. A well conceived multi-channel strategy and operational plan will short-circuit some of this confusion and the potential for mistakes on individual projects.

At the operational level this stage will always require some quick but clear thinking in the following primary areas, linked to which market you are in and what your objectives are.

Segment targeting

Few businesses can afford to offer new channels and to invest in communication indiscriminately. At the outset it is wise to take your understanding of how your customers are segmented and define the scale and focus of initial efforts, including what penetration you are seeking. This can raise the complex issues which we have discussed (customer profitability, channel migration, competitive opportunities, home/office infrastructure, etc.). You need to develop a segment model, along the lines of the discussion in Chapter 4.

Customer recruitment and communication

It is important to target the types of customer who will be receptive to the new services and access mechanisms very carefully. Once you have used research or hypothesis to identify the segments that you are after then you can choose your marketing options – ranging from more promiscuous recruitment approaches, via broadcast media or selected magazines (e.g. *Good Housekeeping*, *GQ*), through to targeting all existing high-value distributors in B2B, or handing a CD registration-kit to specific sets of customers as they purchase from an out-of-town store. Your target customer segments and your recruitment and communications mechanisms must align well. There are many specialist agencies who can help here – just ensure you give them a well-defined brief.

Don't forget that a new online customer will cost between $25 and $75 to recruit and set up, so the better you target them and hold onto them the more profitable you will be. Many businesses give this recruitment activity far too little care and planning – and fail badly as a direct consequence.

Service definition

The service level agreements and broad service requirements that are defined (performance, availability, security, cost constraints, etc.) will impact the choice of partners, technology and implementation options. You are likely to need service agreements with your chosen call-center, payments, warehousing/distribution and online hosting partners. Product or service partners who are being selected to support a broader offer will need formal agreements in exactly the same way. A best-endeavours relationship is always a disaster. The margin, tariffing and charging models will be key to making a profit on every transaction, as we discuss later with the economic model.

Technology and interfaces

Pragmatic solutions are typically needed to provide customers with online self-service browsing, ordering, stock management, track-and-trace, catalog management, personalized pricing and preferencing, added-value information/knowledge services, online promotion/ marketing, service management, money transmission/billing, security, resource management, etc. The mix of these will reflect the service objectives from step 1, and the required integration with existing operations. You must ensure that these online solutions will always "plug and play" with your existing legacy and partner systems. The technical design will be driven by your functional spec and your customer operating model.

Operational plan and partners

Most extended propositions and multi-channel offers will require new operational capabilities and infrastructure. Very often these are not differentiating competencies.

They should therefore be acquired via partners, as we discussed earlier. Operational capabilities and partners here may include technical call-center, contact management center, small-drop or home distribution, integrated marketing, online catalog management, photography, magazine content, online hosting service, etc. Partners can only be selected and in-house operations reconfigured once you have prepared a full functional specification of the service. This is needed in the first four weeks. The specification should summarize in ten pages the range of products, prices, delivery charges, service levels, content responsibilities, access channel priorities, margin proposals, etc. A functional specification states everything very specifically, to flush out disagreement and to shape the beauty contest for partner selection.

Brand and "customer experience" management

Any new relationship channel or service must be aligned with your core promise to your customer and the ability to deliver the promise. The new channels are no different. Big mistakes are often made here. You need to take the main processes in the business and have specialists script how they must work for the customer across all the key access channels. Process maps and traditional storyboards can be bashed out in two weeks if you have the right support team. The secret is to remember what your brand stands for and turn that into a scripted process which governs every major contact with the customer – taking an order, resolving the query, handling a return, driving personal communication, etc.

Linking the channels – integrated operational design

New access and servicing channels must be engineered to build upon existing sales and service channels. Customers will expect an account team to know about their online orders and the call-center to be able to follow up their written enquiry. If the operational design is poor then the overall costs, service problems and customer confusion will get out of hand very quickly. There are again many partners who can help you with this multi-channel operational design.

Step 3: try, learn, improve and exploit

Having agreed a coherent approach you now need to get to market quickly and test the offer – four to six months is a good target.

- The relevant P·R·I·C·E Approach™ components in Step 2 should be rapidly addressed by the project team and a proof-of-concept service set up. A proof-of-concept is a first-cut version of the target operational service. A prototype IT system is required, with minimalist interfaces to existing operations and well designed user interfaces and branding. This can be used to bring the desired operation to life rapidly – using best-of-breed e-services tools which are now available in the market.
- The initial prototype system and creative can be used externally with customer focus groups or via business-to-business interviews, to gain feedback on needs and requirements. A similar approach can be used with functional management across the business to gain ownership and buy-in (something tangible which senior colleagues can touch and understand). The proof-of-concept can be used in the first rollout phase with small trial groups of real customers to test the end-to-end process and operational function.
- Budget for a typical proof-of-concept proposition and set of systems (based on our experience of development and delivery)

would be $300,000 to $600,000 in retail or manufacturing. In areas like financial services the numbers run higher. This would take around four months for the creative, operational design and build, partner selection and then three months to learn from real customers in a pilot implementation. The pilot operation typically is rolled out in one new channel or in one territory, e.g. Chicago.

- The learning from the proof-of-concept work can then be set against a deeper and more robust cut of The P·R·I·C·E Approach™. A cross-functional team would be tasked with developing the operating model for a larger scale service (e.g. 500,000 consumers or 3000 business-to-business customers), with full operations and systems interfaces, high quality customer experience, security and resilience features, recruitment, communication, training etc. Specialist service delivery partners would have been evaluated and selected, to augment internal capabilities. Approval would then be requested for the rollout which would establish customer needs on a wider scale and which would prove the end-to-end service at scale. A further budget here would typically range from $400,000 up to $700,000 for a fully functional service in a wider geography.

- If the initial service is meeting the business objectives and is working well then the wider marketing push and rollout should be taken forward. For new territories, or extensions to the service arising from the trials, there may also be requirements for further operational partners, infrastructures, etc. Costs for this growth phase tend to be relatively linear as scale increases, but at a much lower level than with a traditional operating model. You can typically aim for an international service across Europe, North America or South East Asia within 12–18 months. The limiting factor is often your recruitment of key management with understanding of local supply, logistics, regulatory issues and customer needs.

The general flow of this fast but highly professional process can be represented more simply as shown in Fig. 7.3. This logic flow summarizes the process that we have just gone through.

A tiny amount of structure and focus in your implementation, coupled with avoiding reinventing the wheel (market scanning and the

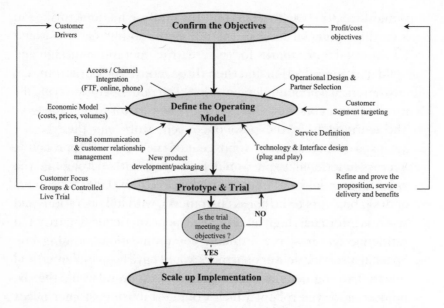

Fig. 7.3 Driving rapid implementation of multi-channel services – the P·R·I·C·E Approach™.

good, the bad and the ugly), will save a typical business a great deal of time and money.

This has all got a bit heavy, but just before we loosen up a little it is worth focusing briefly on how you can ensure that you can turn a buck from these new multi-channel services. If you can bear with this for a little longer, we will have covered how you ensure that your visions and plans can be implemented robustly on the ground and can make money from day one.

The economic model – designing for profit

As we have already said, the new online channels are not discount channels. Adding the Internet and new direct services to your armory does not mean you need to train the shareholder to forget about profit for the next five years. Those who talk about the new-economy bubbles reforming and bursting for ever are of course wrong – but the little bubbles that will continue to burst are those where the sector pioneers have forgotten to drive the basic economics of the service.

In the many e-business projects that we have touched we have evolved a deeply boring set of economic models, which are used to plan the funding of the multi-channel services and to set pricing and service charges at economic but competitive levels. You need to factor in the more expensive customer take-on processes and some higher logistics and infrastructure costs, which are typically then offset by lower servicing, indirects and working capital costs. These models are based upon good old-fashioned spreadsheets, which carry every significant cost and margin associated with these complex supply chains which involve many partners.

To my surprise the models do not vary hugely from sector to sector, but clearly there are always unique balances of cost, margin and price sensitivity. However, they are still founded on the normal business and financial rules which always rely upon the early building of market share and brand building, and must translate rapidly into sustainable gross margin per transaction and shareholder value.

Here are some of the key issues which highlight the changes you must make, to ensure that your multi-channel services are competitive and profitable.

- Loyalty incentives, servicing charges (for the high-cost channels) and customer registration/CRM costs need to be planned differently for the main customer segments. The value of the customers and their potential lifetime contribution must dictate how much you will invest in offering them the widest choices of access and services. The banks have shown everyone the way here – where they often charge low-value customers when they use the high street branch (which costs an order of magnitude more to resolve a query or transfer money than the online self-service channel). The high recruitment costs for some multi-channel services forces you to target which sets of customers to go after – and how you go after them (remember the P·R·I·C·E Approach™).
- The forecast contributions and costs associated with each customer segment must guide the volumes as well as the types of customers you recruit to the new channels and propositions. A

realignment of the marketing budget must follow. Ensure that the spend on general brand-building and broadcast communication (e.g. TV ads) is balanced by the one-to-one budgets. I do feel that a lot of the new Internet signposting money can be wasted – where some companies give inappropriate and almost random amounts to AOL or Amazon, just to be in the game. Many people who don't remember to visit your Website won't respond to an AOL signpost. Far better to remind them about your online services on the doorstep, as you deliver goods or when they visit your high street store.

- A good economic and marketing model can help the management team to weigh cause and effect. The key sensitivities in a multi-channel model are subtly different from a traditional business model. The details are too dry to flesh out here – but I can summarize briefly. The big sensitivities which we find time and time again are:

  - The cannibalization level of customers recruited to new channels from the existing channels, i.e. stealing customers from your own retail operations.

  - Customer penetration, order size for direct or home delivery and delivery versus collection levels (for physical products such as groceries or wine and spirits).

  - Returns rate (a new area for many businesses, where 30% of products can bounce back at huge cost, fulfillment/delivery charge, assortment spread, working capital ...).

  - Customer care ratios (e.g. the percentage of queries or telephone orders which come into a call-centre as a result of 100 orders).

  - First-mover media effect, versus second-mover marketing costs. Amazon received up to $20bn of free advertising in every newspaper and seminar over the last three years. Only first-movers get this dividend. Those who come in second have to invest much more to get the same share of voice.

  - Traditional servicing cost replacement, order frequency and uptake of added-value profit services – you buy my home services, so why not take a loan, buy a holiday, etc. Margins are usually much higher with add-on products. If the average

I haven't quite worked out how so many businesses like *Encyclopaedia Britannica* and a range of newspapers offer their content free on the Web, whereas they used to cost £2000 or 50c on paper. If you can work this out please let me know. In more tangible markets the rules of profitability and relationship management are much clearer – so make sure your people learn them without delay.

customer uses two or three services rather than just one, you do much better.

The operating models that successful online businesses use for service design tend to zero in very precisely on many of these sensitivities. If you want to engineer your services for profit, I would urge you to get your management accountants involved early. Ensure that they understand how to feed the big sensitivities into the service design, pricing, marketing plans, launch priorities, recruitment targeting, etc.

Now is probably a good time for a cup of coffee and a lie down. We have gone through the challenges, the strategies, the planning approaches, the way to short-cut the lessons of others and the way to get it right in the market at a profit.

In the next chapter we get to the organization thing – which can be a further stretch for businesses used to doing it all in the ways that have worked well for 20 years.

Chapter 8

Transforming the Organization and "Living the Brand"

In a multi-channel business a few age-old principles scream out as loudly as they have ever done.

- Your people and the key staff that you rely upon in partners are vital to the feel of the brand and the day-to-day service to customers. They meet them on high streets, talk to them via the phone, program and respond to the online dialog and define the service level agreements, which dictate the tone and nature of the customer experience.
- If you cannot meet customers' expectations right first time, your clever technology will go the same way as Boo and a thousand other famous e-commerce failures.
- Basic product performance and your innovation culture is still pivotal. A flexible set of multi-channel operations, which provide second-best products to your door at the touch of a new age mobile device, is OK, but it will soon be outflanked when customers start talking to each other. We are in an age where people and processes need to have a high metabolic rate. Moves in the market by competitors can be picked up quickly and must be reacted to even faster than you drive your own inventions. There are a mix of old and new lessons to be learnt, about how your people work together if you are to stay ahead of the pack with great products and services.
- Businesses will need great technology people and IT specialists, who can ensure that new capabilities and opportunities are constantly being filtered and factored into current thinking. You

will continue to see a good acceleration effect over the next five years if you can harness these people and their specialized knowledge for your business. This is not about creating business and IT hybrids any more – your business managers really ought to have general IT awareness by now (if not – keep panicking). This is about developing real specialists who can see through the technology fog to bring products like SpeechWorks to your door, (at last a usable voice-activated electronic service is here after waiting 20 years).

So let's go through some of these big organizational and people things, which will give your new strategy and plans a fighting chance of being delivered.

I will start with a little experience of "living the brand" from Gap, which sets the tone nicely for the attitude we are looking for across face-to-face, telephone and the full range of online channels.

A friend of ours from Australia moved back home recently. There isn't a Gap store in Melbourne, so when she went into our local store just before she left she bemoaned this fact to a member of staff. The staff member immediately offered to post any products that she wanted to her in Australia if she phoned or e-mailed the details. Our friend was of course hugely impressed by the attitude and spirit of the Gap staff, who have clearly been very well trained. One would hope that the local staff would be able to draw on a standard Gap infrastructure to manage this offer cost-effectively, but we may never know. I think that the point is a simple one. You must get your Internet and your multi-channel act together fast, but don't forget that your brand is still your most prized asset and that a big part of your interface to customers may still be face-to-face. Don't forget the loyalty that you can create by surpassing expectation. Don't ever dilute your brand values on the high street or on the doorstep, or no one will believe your promises in the direct channels.

When Gap announce that they are introducing maternity wear which is only available on the Web I see another glimpse of a multi-channel business who is getting its act together in some very smart ways.

So live the brand at all levels and be prepared to spend as much money on staff training and communication as on fancy new interactive systems.

Now let's look at what you might spend some of that training money on.

Serving the customer – right first time

This is a boring sort of magic, but it is allowing leading businesses to deconstruct the main processes which serve the customer and to equip staff to be very fleet of foot and efficient, on behalf of the customer.

I find that the majority of retail and manufacturing businesses are valiantly struggling to answer a series of really important questions, but so often in a piecemeal and highly confusing way:

- How can I guarantee a great customer experience in my direct services (home shopping, workplace services, etc.) to match the service in my current "bricks-and-mortar" channels?
- How can we support this range of different products and services for different consumer segments without bankrupting the company? Complexity usually adds cost and it can confuse everyone, including the staff.
- How can I ensure operationally that we use the new infrastructure to deliver a richer and closer relationship with the customer and an effective set of services to support it? How can we provide an intimate and personalized service whenever they touch us?

The leading businesses who make this journey cost-effectively have all cracked one particular secret. They focus ruthlessly on redesigning the most important interactions with the customer and transforming how they work across the channels. It is like the old "right first time" crusade, where what sounded like an expensive commitment to service actually reduces cost dramatically down through the service chain.

The approach that is needed is one of the dullest things in the world to focus on for many marketeers and innovators, yet it is a basic essential if a company is to ride the new consumer waves cost-effectively. It is about creating and implementing an *integrated operational design*, which spans the critical processes which serve the customer and which turns the customer operating model into a practical reality. We mentioned this in the P·R·I·C·E Approach™ in Chapter 7. This is not about engaging a huge consultancy exercise that creates a monumental library of process maps and gobbledygook. It is about creating a tightly focused and simple operational blueprint, which evolves a business from its historical operations and structures so that it can serve the customer efficiently, across a range of channels.

The precise approach and operational solutions will vary for different types of business. They all hinge on understanding the key processes and "transactions" which customers rely upon every day across the current and new channels, irrespective of the product or service they choose. In simple terms – what do your customers need to work best – what are their priorities?

For a bank, for example, the customer needs easy access to cash, account balances and statement information across all channels (branch, phone, mail, Internet). If they move house they want to write to the bank only once, across all seven product divisions. This sounds easy but many banks still can't offer it – because of the way that they are structured internally on product lines. Many businesses who grow by acquisition have exactly the same problem. Customers also don't want to be offered products that they already have or could never afford. If a customer writes to you on Monday, they expect your call-center to know about this recent mail inquiry on Thursday and to be able to talk about progress on addressing it. Can your business guarantee this type of integrated relationship?

A good example of the approach you should adopt can be taken from the general retail sector, which illustrates the approach that I believe all businesses should go through.

1   First pick out the big operational or service wins for the customer which your multi-channel strategy and research tells you will improve loyalty, convenience and repeat purchase (and those which will eliminate most cost for you). These customer benefits

should tie in with the overall customer experience which fall out of your multi-channel strategy.

2 Identify at the same time the handful of relationship processes which are fundamental to product and service delivery and building sales across existing and new channels.

Examples of key relationship processes may include:

- keeping target customers informed about products they should be interested in (and they can just say yes to, to trigger product set up or delivery, i.e. they have been pre-approved);
- returns processes and essential complaints/query handling;
- management of pricing, discounts, promotion – relevant to each category and customer segment;
- product or service bundling, where individual component of services or products are tailored to personal needs;
- maintenance of important customer data, including customer identification/security which can be used in any channel, preferred delivery method, default payment details and address; and
- payments processing.

The plethora of internal and minor back-office, administrative and logistics processes which are not central to the customer experience or product/service delivery must not play a big role in creating the operational framework. *If you do not enforce a 20/80 focus on this (the few things which make most impact) you will disappear into a vortex of process mapping and IT ballet – which will hold you at the bottom of the sea for eight years.*

3 The framework and priorities identified in steps 1 and 2 will vary from business to business, but a shrewd and experienced eye must now be used to create an overall operational architecture and roadmap for the procedures and information systems. This will chart how these key customer interactions and product processes will work efficiently across the channels and at scale in this new world. The designs will then impact the shape of every new project.

Yes – this does mean some minimalist process maps/flows, and a range of detailed changes to staff procedures, systems interfaces and the way some key activities get done. This includes where products and services are managed by central organizations and via the different access channels. The payback of course is that customers can use the same password on the Website as they use with the call-center, and a wide range of other simple benefits and efficiencies.

It sounds really dull doesn't it? It sounds like it will take a year and will cost $3m or more. Well actually it can often be crashed through in 8–12 weeks, if you focus ruthlessly on only the major interactions which make all the difference to your customer and affect the cost-base the most. A number of the boutique consultancies who focus on customer relationship management should be able to help your people if they risk getting lost in the bushes. You will soon have a business design which you can use to drive changes in operational procedures, service design for outsource partners and systems design to help shape your lead projects so that you can capture the benefits – step by step.

4   Don't try to eat the hippopotamus in one go – build your new ambitions to service customers more coherently step by step, project by project.

In the early new-economy years, a typical board of a company would decide to do something about the Internet and e-commerce, whatever that is (they thought back then). Very often one of the board members, let's call him Derek, will have a passion to get something out there fast. Most of his colleagues will think it is all a half-baked waste of time. To shut Derek up and to seem willing, the board will typically have agreed a modest or immodest sum to be spent, without setting any particular context in terms of customer, product or sales objectives. The embarrassing fiasco in the market was born that day. The carbuncle that duplicated all of the customer interactions in a disconnected way was born that day.

Unless Derek is switched on to a right-first-time approach, using a sensible rapid development approach (Chapter 7) and a good understanding of likely quick wins, he will end up with a pathetic knee-jerk offering and a horrible set of customer services – just as we have seen in the good, the bad and the ugly. The services will not meet customer needs and won't be adequately integrated with other channels.

The operating model and the integrated operational design tells you how you should be servicing the customer most flexibly and cost-effectively across current and emerging. The trick is to use your change agenda to reshape or realign the existing projects that you have agreed already, so that you can grab chunks of the benefits as cost-effectively and quickly as possible. There will be gaps to fill, but it is remarkable how often you can accelerate a coherent set of next-generation operations within a year or two, by intercepting and amending existing projects.

You will need an aggressive character who will own and police the integrated design and staff training on the ground, to cut through the defensive garbage you will encounter.

As we touched upon earlier, customers usually expect the left arm to know what the right arm is doing. They will ring in one day, visit a branch the next and come in to the new online service from their office the next. They don't expect perfection, but questions like "Where is my order?" cannot be met with a blank stare in an alternative channel. I could bore you to death on the wide range of ridiculous potholes which the knee-jerkers fall into. They usually put the cause back two years, because the conservative plodders in other parts of the organization can say "We have tried it, but our customers are not ready for it yet." In the absence of knowledge and a design, Derek will simply often put a paper catalog or a service/price list into electronic form and pretend that he is testing a revolutionary new customer proposition.

It is like sailing off for the New World across the Pacific in an enormous canoe.

If you can act now to intercept these expensive and poorly designed services you can typically build some of the core "customer facing" capabilities efficiently, to meet the immediate needs of the project and serving the wider purpose. Some of Derek's projects in multinational businesses may have a $2m budget or more – so for them there is often a lot of cash to play with already.

But getting the design and integration with existing channel and retail operations right at the outset is much slower isn't it? Won't you risk losing first-mover advantage? Not a bit of it. I know a number of implementations which cost a fraction of those of their competitors.

The difference between supermarkets Tesco's and Sainsbury's forays into home-shopping in the UK is a great example. Both had the odd drama initially, but Tesco were apparently much more in command of what they were doing. They spent a lot less time and money building their online services and have since dramatically outperformed the innovation of Sainsbury from all angles (in the eyes of the customers and certainly in my opinion). Sainsbury are now plotting the fight back – so we will see who wins the next round. They seem to have outsourced their IT activities to Andersen, which is not really the reaction I was expecting from them.

A similar comparison can be made between Hannafords and Walmart in the US. Walmart moved more cautiously and got their act together before they made their moves. Hannafords set up homeruns as a separate operation and then ultimately sold it off, prior to it drifting into obscurity.

They came to market quickly because they knew what they were doing and they paused briefly to choose the right tools for the job. The P·R·I·C·E Approach™ we mentioned earlier illustrates how speed needn't be compromised if you go for well structured initiatives – it is a matter of getting the priorities clear.

I guarantee that if you get your act together you will be able to put sophisticated products and wonderful new e-commerce offerings together far more cheaply than, and just as quickly as, the panic-inspired standalone carbuncle which pops up in left field. You also avoid baffling the customer with a blizzard of incompatible services – or four different numbers to ring in the same organization when the customer moves house and wants to record an address change.

Getting your products to market faster

It is remarkable how large businesses can sometimes fail to produce any meaningful innovation for extended periods, despite having an army of bright people clogging up their expensive offices and laboratories. The new business-to-business exchanges, financial supermarkets showing product comparisons and the blizzard of best-buy Internet sites will make service and product specification, performance and value comparison easier than ever before. There is a real step-change going on in the broking model and the ability of word of mouth to echo around the world. Your products will be measured against twenty others from here to Timbuktu – so you had better benchmark well.

Innovation has always been a priority in most businesses, but there have always been some natural barriers to a strong flow of innovation which help businesses meet both the old benchmarks and the new ones. There are typically three types of barriers in place in many businesses, and the need for a number of essential ingredients to overcome them and to unleash the great ideas buried within the business. These ideas and approaches have been developed over many years, from working with and observing some of the most innovative businesses in the world.

Let's take the barriers first.

Problem number one is the inability to decide what should get priority and what should not. Product ideas which are half-starved of resources never make it to the market. The fences are too high and the market moves on if the new ideas take too long to progress, so they get recycled back for various bits of rework. They never get the full resources they ask for but they never also get nothing at all (allowing another project to be fully resourced). If you cannot apply ruthless prioritization, i.e. feed some projects and stop others, then you will ultimately fail at almost everything. This is what happens in lots of big businesses. The most common reason that this can happen is that the CEO or the development director does not have the balls to get the senior team to sit down and work as a team to make the hard priority calls. The CEO also does not have a process to help this prioritization debate. Processes for this exist and work really well in even the most complex businesses – but for some baffling reason most businesses are still poor at innovation and cannot manage this brutal type of focus, irrespective of the quality of their people.

Problem number two is the thought-police or "the permafrost layer," who often reside in the lesser board positions and in the senior management level below. The great innovators of 10–20 years ago and the unimaginative young fogies, who may want to curry favor as having "wisdom beyond their years," will gently use the bureaucratic process to pour glycerine around the innovation process. Things slip, resource gets diverted, decisions get looped and deferred, more research is needed, external solutions and partners get challenged (we could do better in-house). The very valid goal of "right first time," "more speed less haste" gets cleverly corrupted into the pursuit of great acetates and pretty presentations, while nothing new really happens on the ground.

This one is pretty easy to stop, but it requires the CEO to ensure that her own thoughts and ambition are correctly focused and thought through. She must then ensure that the forces of darkness are put back in their box. Someone who is always pouring "the voice of reality" into decisions, but never personally accelerates anything needs to be sacked, for the good of all. Let them go and screw up someone else while you get on with building the future.

People with good instincts, who can make quick decisions and tend to be right most of the time, are the only people that you want in influential positions.

The third barrier is usually the very structure of the business. We talked earlier about the flexible operating model and the need to use external partners for non-differentiating activities, so that the internal people could manage and innovate the things that matter most. If your business is fundamentally constrained in the way that the whole supply chain works and customers are serviced then it is always hard to innovate. Some businesses spend a fortune on researching new manufacturing and packaging innovations. They don't realise that customer knowledge, accessibility and only one or two areas of product performance are really competitive differentiators. The trick is to diagnose this problem clearly and not confuse it with the other two problems.

The radical solution to this problem can be to find flexible outsource partners for back-office, call-center/customer care operations, supply/manufacturing, procurement or the other functions which are not central to your unique sales proposition. If your organization and competencies are not really your problem, but you have to outsource to get rid of the permafrost layer of management, then you really have more serious management and leadership problems than anything else.

So let's turn to the solutions which any serious business should use to foster innovation.

The first ingredient is to aim for a good balance between innovations which customers will see and projects which cut your internal costs. Put all of your projects into a matrix which highlights to the board the mix of customer-perceived innovation and implementation difficulty. The example in Fig. 8.1 shows how a retailer's portfolio might look.

Map your major projects and investment spend using this chart. An innovation-led business must see lots of projects clustered on the high impact side, but with a good sprinkling at the easier level (smart innovation which customers value and is low cost can often come from repackaging existing services, with perhaps a new channel or self-service angle). Such quick wins can be just as hard to emulate in poorly structured competitors as the extremely difficult or risky projects. This is where a flexible product hub is worth its weight in gold.

An innovation led business must not forget operational efficiency. But they will expect back-office projects there to be offering significant

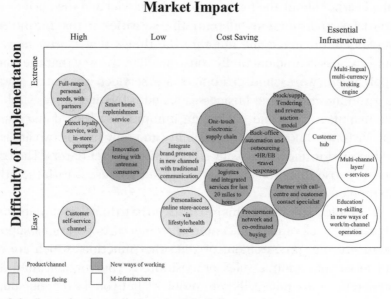

Fig. 8.1 Example of a retailer's project portfolio.

cost-savings, rather than self-indulgent functional projects with spurious or weak benefits.

Too many infrastructure projects means that you need to get outsourcing fast, or your whole resource pool will be consumed by painting fences and keeping up with back-office regulatory changes that customers don't care about.

The second ingredient is to change the way that you run projects, so that teams are empowered to deliver the goods and plans are signed off at fewer (but more rigorously applied) decision points. There are many classical project "funnels" which innovation-led businesses use to weed out the stronger ideas and apply resource to them aggressively. In Unilever, the team communication processes that we introduced on the back of an early version of an intranet were really the key to helping teams to accelerate projects, and to ensure that ideas and contributions could flow fairly freely across a very large enterprise. A well designed intranet-based project and teamworking system will pay for itself one thousand times over. I have seen a number of environments across blue-chip and fast-moving businesses where the IT infrastructure is designed to support the project teams to co-ordinate actions and progress in real-time. They offer a great way to avoid the classical confusions, which slow most projects down or push them off the rails.

The third ingredient is the implementation of the customer operating model and the product hub – which will unleash the full inventive forces in the business to provide breathtaking customer innovation, in terms of function, performance and convenience. There are few innovation-led businesses which are really successful who are not living by these general rules, in one form or another. There are also lots of modestly successful businesses who are really hitting the buffers because they have mysteriously overlooked one of these building blocks or missed the obvious solutions. Marks & Spencer in the UK are a great example – a business that is one of the best retailers in the world but who appeared a few years ago to have locked itself into a moribund set of approaches, with a layer of permafrost management that was killing the reinvention of the business model. I met one of their second-tier directors in M&S in mid-1998 and there was all of the trademark smugness, cynicism and self-righteous conservatism that one might have expected. I haven't bothered to find out whether he survived the bloodbath a year later, when M&S hit the wall and had a clear out. In the last six months the humility and vision has set in at a grassroots level and I have marked the share as a buy once more (with some trepidation).

These are things that companies can easily test themselves on by asking their suppliers what they think about them. Try this yourself. Bring a handful of your suppliers together, ranging from commodity and service suppliers through to technical and business consultants. Ask them to do a simple blind assessment of your culture and effectiveness as they individually see it.

Are you receptive to new ideas? Are your brightest thinkers encouraged to experiment? Do you benchmark well in terms of speed of decision making and shared understanding of priorities? Ply your suppliers with alcohol and discuss the headlines openly – you will find it very insightful. It is not a statistically reliable process, but it does allow warning bells to ring if your partners don't feel that they are invited to help you innovate or feel you have cultural problems that you haven't spotted yourselves. They will often be more balanced in their feedback than internal people, as long as you give them permission to be candid and keep them away from their personal areas of sales opportunity.

Building a progressive and ambitious culture

This brings us nicely onto what to do about cultural change. Creating and developing a multi-channel business which can innovate along a whole range of axes requires a very informed, trained and engaged management and staff. Events which first influenced my thinking about changing culture were the "oh be joyful" jamborees and the global roadshows I got involved with at Unilever and Barclays. The "oh be joyful" was a big international gathering of the higher echelons in Unilever once a year (a few hundred taken from 300,000 total employees). It was a generally boring plod in the afternoon, with the chairmen providing an update of the year gone by and the year to come. It was done with typical Anglo-Dutch sangfroid (no razzle and American style exhortation) – all very low key. The evening was then a black-tie, smoke-filled bonding session, where you met old mates, had a leisurely skinful and fell into bed at the Dorchester to sleep it off. I used to love the evening do. Over seven or eight consecutive years I was never disappointed by the glow it left. All I was really doing was reinforcing a personal network, which I then exploited to get things done during the year.

The formal part of the day was really a shameful waste of hugely expensive brainpower. It was usually neither especially informative or even interesting or motivational. It also felt a little elitist and stuffy, without being much fun – and it probably alienated a huge bunch of people who never quite made it to one. But, the networking and buzz later, particularly after midnight, remains an object lesson in cultural glue. Similar events and networking processes also took place at lower levels across functions and geographies. Despite their shortcomings they formed a key part of what made Unilever so formidable as an organization.

At Barclays it was much more hierarchical. The formal group events were usually less fun also. The most enjoyable events were slightly off to one side, such as the big bash that Andersen ran in London, which often finished in the clubs. Then Richard Rae-Smith, the head of retailing banking (my boss) and his wondrous PA, Nigel, pulled together the Power-of-one events. As directors we all were given tasks to perform at a series of huge events which were run for tranches of staff from across the retail businesses. Our roles involved communication of the vision and plans, with carefully choreographed elements of public humiliation for us senior types. It was great – a world apart from the more pedestrian and patronizing "old bank" communications and events which were the norm.

I thoroughly enjoyed my compèring role, although the "stand-up" component (stand-up in the metaphorically and literal sense) resulted in me needing a serious massage in the hotel by the final day, to take my mind off the lower back pain. Young Nigel kindly organized it, but I really didn't enjoy it much. I had never had a massage before and I was on tenterhooks all the time waiting for the nice lady to offer me something which I would find hugely embarrassing. Most men are still little boys really. I plead guilty to that, and I would like five other charges to be taken into consideration. I think that the massage helped a bit, although I cannot say that I enjoyed it at all.

I digress though. I think these showcase "emotional" events were in no way extravagant in an organization with 35,000 coalface staff. You can't mobilize a community unless you generate a great deal of passion, shared understanding and commitment. Complex visions and plans which transform how you deal with customers will only work if they are forcibly distilled into simple and memorable communications, which staff can understand and will continue to motivate them in the days and months to come.

In an environment like Barclays, with lots of petty fiefdoms and furtive turf wars, it also should publicly bind and commit people to the cause – which in this case was a very compelling mission to create a step-change in how we served customers. I would strongly recommend these types of communication efforts for these reasons. I have been involved in quite a number since and they are worth their weight in gold. But only do them if you can brand them and focus the content. Ensure that the senior management take personal ownership – they perform better than anyone expects and the junior staff are normally amazed to see that they can be touchingly human and even engaging. Hierarchical power without some additional emotional forces is like chicken madras without the curry powder – it works in a basic way but it doesn't fire you up.

If you decide to go for the "improve the proposition" or "change the market" strategies you will definitely need to organize an all-encompassing education and communication process. You should make these events as much fun and be as engaging as possible – or your grand vision which will guarantee your survival of the m-bomb will appear like all the usual communication activities that introduce every new fashion.

At one Power-of-one conference we even managed to get all twelve of us who were speaking to casually drop the word "Lilliputian" into our speeches somewhere. Even boring bankers drink too much and make strange and ridiculous pacts in the dark hours. We had agreed this challenge in the bar at one a.m. the previous night. Everyone managed it one way or the other, mostly in the right context – although the guy in charge of mortgages was so proud of himself when he snuck the word in that he immediately forgot the rest of his sentence. It was no Lilliputian achievement for a bunch of suits to be so human – and we even got a few complaints from a few stuffed shirts in the audience.

On a different tack I have been impressed by the businesses who are looking to countries like the Phillipines, who are providing 170,000 computer science and accounting graduates a year to blue-chips around the world. They are used by companies like Barnes & Noble (supply-chain services/purchasing), P&G and Alitalia (for accounting) and Caltex. At US $5.50 per day they are proving to be a useful cultural and cost driver for these businesses – in a number of ways.

See if your senior team has the daftness or competitive spirit to do something as subtly ridiculous at one of your events. Only four staff out of a thousand who noticed our Lilliputian efforts objected on their feedback forms – so I presume the rest may have even appreciated the spontaneity. I was tempted to get a handwriting expert to track down the humorless characters who complained, and have them posted to look after the replenishment of ATMs in Iceland.

Using technology and IT leaders to add oxygen and Semtex to the mix

We know that technology advances can introduce a new channel opportunity every six months. We also know that ten other siren voices pop up during the same period to divert you from the one true path. The trick is to spot which is which! I am afraid I must turn briefly to a story from my time in Unilever in the early 1990s, which I think provides some excellent lessons for today. It was also such an extraordinary experience at the time.

Mike Johnson was a top-ranking commercial guy who was sponsored by the group chairman to grab IT by the scruff of the neck in the early 1990s. Some £400m per annum was spent by 4000 IT staff scattered across 75 countries. If any two of the 500 operating units were using the same IT package, infrastructure and tools then that was largely coincidental. If it were to happen by accident then one of the two companies would probably switch to a new solution on a point of principle. We would say this as our little joke but it was really very close to the truth.

Mike rang me up in Animal Feeds, out of the blue, and dragged me in to help decide what needed doing and then to create some sort of revolution. Mike's goal was to bring technology into the heart of the business reinvention that he felt was long overdue. We knew that the competitive storm clouds were gathering and that technology was poised to have a huge impact on most ways that we would compete in the future. A guy called Martin Armitage who looked after IT in the Foods businesses was an immediate partner in crime, and we embarked upon creating a radical new business vision and IT architecture which would grab people's attention and aim to transform how Unilever worked. Within three months we had a draft set of business prizes identified in supply chain, customer management and product innovation. We developed these agendas from discussions with key senior managers and power-brokers, where they could see a compelling argument for change, as well as from our insights into where technology could release huge efficiencies.

We then just had to convince a few thousand of the senior people across the business that the vision for the new ways of co-ordinating and driving IT, and networking the organization, would deliver these benefits.

In parallel with these aggressive business debates, Martin and I traveled the world, and worked with the engineers of the primary suppliers of business applications and software to define technology architecture and a set of tools which would ensure three things.

Our first goal was that any development in one country had to be able to be rapidly used and exploited in another, without them having to throw out their existing stack of systems. Secondly, a global information-sharing model and set of solutions were needed, so that all 300,000 Unilever staff could potentially work together in remote electronic teams, to deliver the business prizes desk to desk, without technology differences and time and distance getting in the way. Thirdly, Unilever needed to extract huge benefits in dealings with suppliers, from simple savings on IT components to achieving competitive leverage with suppliers who could help develop advanced business solutions for us. All the above had to "plug and play" with advanced business approaches that we would need to evolve in order to deliver the hard business benefits – fast.

A network of the senior IT players around the world gradually formed. Our choices were made for open systems platforms (Unix, available from all our key hardware partners, and Microsoft on the desktop, linked using Internet protocols), office tools, database, development tools, etc. External stars were brought in to join the central team – David Smith from a premier management consultancy and Nick White, a world telecoms leader from Midland Bank. More internal stars joined the crusade (Ed Ball, now at Novartis, and Grahame Wright, now a director with Halifax Bank and Luc Cloet – a charming Belgian generalist). We took the whole business-to-technology show on the road to get the buy-in and feedback from the IT community in months four to six from the initial get-go.

In some geographies we received critical but genuine agreement. In others we encountered either severe but positive challenge, or stunned confusion and entrenched opposition. We made some mistakes here, and definitely were too arrogant and overpowering. Most of this stuff was completely new and came out of left field for many of our people. We didn't give the detractors any quarter. As a result we later suffered pockets of inertia where we hadn't used common sense and patience to win people over.

Many IT shops in the large operating companies had been making their own decisions since the dawn of time. They were great at running huge infrastructures and mainframes, with all the specialized skills and the large numbers of support people that they required. One particular session with all the US IT heads turned into a bloodbath – with them telling us we were dangerously wrong and misguided. We ended up effectively telling some of the guys that they had no choice if they wanted a job. I learned a lot during this period about how to ensure that radical changes could go in fast, but also about how to be just a little smarter in reducing heat, confusion and ownership. We got some of the people issues badly wrong, but we had enough momentum and sponsorship to flick the dinosaur's tail.

Mike was particularly focused because he was living with the time bomb of cancer. He had always been very direct and action orientated, but by this time Mike was in a period of remission in a cycle which was already well past the point where the doctors thought he would still be around. Mike was a man of huge personal courage and he was an object lesson in simplicity, clarity and the leadership thing. Mike would have loved the challenge of the m-bomb, and would have ensured that his business got to the Promised Land.

Martin and I were still young at the time and also suffered from an overdose of conviction and confidence. It was good that the wider team has a broader mix of tones to provide a softer edge here and there. Our vision for the business, and our technology and solutions plans for the global business, encompassed a revolution in ways of working for all staff, unlimited connectivity and reusability of systems and innovations across all divisions. It was actually founded on the early Internet stack, but unfortunately could not use the tools of the World Wide Web yet, or tools like Broadvision, e-speak or Siebel. We had little idea how the full power of the Internet would really grow until we caught a glimpse through Iain Anderson, our main board director.

I will always remember a discussion I had with Iain in Florida in 1993, when he told me how his son was seeing the Internet revolution unfold, from the relative safety of his New England college. Iain challenged me all those years ago on how our grand vision was going to transition to the much greater opportunities and challenges presented by the Web. At the time I couldn't even answer the question intelligently, and spent the next two weeks quietly scrabbling to work out what he was getting excited about. It soon became clear how the reach of what we were doing could evolve.

Through this period we were crafting and evolving a vision to give Unilever staff, businesses and partners the private competitive edge and the flexibility that today's Internet now gives everybody – large and small. It was no wonder it took some of the corners of the business a while to get it. We also certainly suffered here and there when we underestimated the challenge of changing such a behemoth.

Within 12 months we had created a real bush fire and the whole IT landscape had changed. The new development and architecture approaches were underway in lead countries, with leadership of different world-class business solutions and package implementations now federated to lead businesses around the world. We were learning all the time about hearts and minds and how to employ and motivate the 4000 IT people in the smartest way. We had global deals with a range of companies like SAP and Oracle in place, and prices were tumbling down as we leveraged our buying power.

We branded the business programs of change around the UNISON brand – UNISON meant new ways to manage brands, innovate products, serve customers and communicate with each other across the organization.

We used every speaking platform and personal relationship we could to engage all the business community in UNISON. We made videos, showing how it would help you to co-design and innovate new products across time zones, keeping innovation rolling 24 hours a day with the sun. The global e-mail solutions were on everyone's desk within a further 6–12 months, linking virtually every manager in the business from Bangalore to Beijing.

Niall FitzGerald, who headed up the Detergents business (and is now the chairman of Unilever), started telling people that if you e-mailed him he would respond within a day – if you wrote to him it may take up to a week. The main levers of cultural change and step-change of IT exploitation were all lined up in a row. Most of the key people saw the win and it happened. Unilever got lost once or twice in the foothills but staggered at last into base camp in the information society. We stepped up to serious challenges, such as regional implementation of supply-chains and manufacturing networks across operating units, using the same SAP engines. We took the opportunity during the journey to bring together the brands and consumer offers across the territories, using new information flows and approaches to help the new organization develop.

Whilst we had our ups and downs I have never seen a community blossom so much as our IT guys did during Mike Johnson's era. What was a low-key and highly fragmented support function grew dramatically in confidence and shared purpose. Much of the progress was on internal processes and efficiencies, rather than today's extended multi-channel models, but it was still a great crusade to be part of.

I would recommend the following approaches for any IT organization in a large, fast-moving business. They have since been tested and refined, as we work with many businesses which are now having to make six-month projects and high competitive impact the norm.

1   Break up your big all-encompassing projects into sensible chunks which can typically be delivered in six to nine months. If it is planned to take over a year or cost $10m, I can guarantee it will

be a disappointing mess – the project will lose focus, momentum and buy-in and the world will move on. The only exceptions to this rule are huge replacements of trading engines in financial services or complete replacements of integrated manufacturing systems. Should you be focusing on these monolithic projects anyway, given what is happening in the markets?

2   In any international business, where P&L responsibility is held locally, there will always be strong local agendas to balance with the global agendas.

As a rule of thumb, the regional and global agenda (and synergies in shared partners and developments) need to get the dominant share of investment now. Additionally you should be spending a least twice as much on global lead projects and infrastructures than you were two years ago. In a number of successful businesses this has gone to ten times as much.

3   Global lead projects should initially always be federated out around the lead local businesses. Projects led by head office are slow and bureaucratic, and tend to lose touch with practical business and customer needs. People in head offices have also typically evolved past the point where they can do anything practical or useful any more. Guaranteeing reusability of the systems is all about rewarding the development team in the lead operating company for the second and third deployment in other countries – and choosing the right people and project structures in the first place.

4   All the major components of your global shared operating model should be multi-channel and designed to support modern ways of working and innovating. They should be tied together with business logic (endorsed by functional leaders, via heavy negotiation) and put into a powerful marketing and communication framework. Put a team together who can draw out the full stack of business design, operations processes and IT architecture/solutions, and then discuss and agree with key colleagues worldwide. You can do this in six to nine months – in any business, however large. The core options are easier now and the technology capability has stepped even further ahead of your culture and ways of working in most businesses today (so almost everything you go for will be proven somewhere).

5   Your technology people need to have great communication skills and business instinct, as well as a strong technology and implementation nose. Pay what you need to pay for key people – a weak manager can cost you $10m a year (or per month in financial services).

6   Speed of action is more important than purity of decision. 80% is good enough. Don't agonize too long over which multi-channel middleware or payment system to use – just choose one which is good enough and you can touch and feel.

Driving new ways of working and managing the matrix

To continue my Unilever story, I then was asked to join the Detergents Executive (the board of the global £8bn detergent business) to help use these tools and capabilities to transform how we drove innovation, managed brands, sourced products and served customers across the world. From my personal viewpoint it sounded a bit like having your bluff called. OK, so you have talked about it and promised it – let's do it. After some steep learning curves, our targeted use of advanced information and systems played an important role in achieving some of these step-changes, including tactical things such as saving £400m per annum in raw material costs, through co-ordinating buying across the world. The new innovation process and systems that we introduced were able to leverage our R&D expertise and creative ideas of 75 countries, without having to unpick the strange matrix organization.

Unilever has always had an interwoven matrix of product groups, geographies and functions. Country managers with P&L responsibility had to master and integrate the brand processes and supply chains which came with the three international product businesses – Foods, Detergents and Personal Products. I often hear matrix management used as an excuse for the failure of large businesses to gain synergies – or to move quickly. I think that this is complete nonsense. Businesses don't move quickly if there is either no leadership, no culture of working together, no aggressive agenda to focus the minds or no understanding of that agenda down through the business. Matrices will always be there in an international business with many product groups. Managing matrix reporting and organization is also a key skill in a multi-channel business – but the axes of invention and management become those of customer, product and channel (functional management really should be subordinated). I learnt all those years ago that the trick is to set up and manage the key 20/80 processes and information flows which need to cut through the matrix, e.g. things like innovation projects, brand development, procurement and elements of customer or consumer management. The level of interference in the remaining 80% of things that local managers need to just get on with must be close to zero. If you get this balance wrong you will fail miserably – and at high cost.

We agreed these priorities for new ways of working and big prizes from the use of IT within the global executive. We then worked with the local teams to pull together a radically new "operating model" and processes which would deliver the objectives in each area. We used lead country IT teams and some fast-moving external partners to create sexy and very friendly teamworking systems to support each global process within six months. It was amazingly quick – and it showed how big change agendas and multi-billion dollar prizes or brand leverage agendas could help kick parochial interests and defense mechanisms out of the way. If you operate in a complex business I would recommend this powerful approach of strategy → prizes → 20/80 processes → teamworking and IT → quick wins → cultural reinforcement → big wins.

Buy-in, bush fires and mid-life crises

To get the communication and shared understanding working, the executive presented the overall vision and plans to all the chairmen from around the world, in Florida. For my part, I did a dog and pony show with the sexier end of the international strategy and technology approaches – Steven Spielberg meets Nick Negroponte. Having secured the buy-in of the top brass I then took a roadshow out to the Unilever companies in 25 countries on six continents over four months, talking through the business strategy, operational approach, and then getting people's hands on with the tools and technologies. No major change will ever take root unless you capture hearts and minds and communicate, communicate, communicate.

Research across hundreds of companies tells us that in most businesses the average middle manager has no ideas what the strategy is, so you need to get out there if you want to make the elephant dance.

The road-show almost killed us, but we got loads of great feedback as well as a huge kick-start to the process. On the downside I picked up a bout of dysentery in one country, which stayed with me like an unwelcome lodger for several weeks (a funny story for another day). I also re-learned that when some nationalities nod their heads vigorously it doesn't mean that they agree with you – it just means that they have successfully translated what you have just said.

On one fateful day in Japan I reached a personal crisis, when I realized I was losing the sparkle of youth. It was my first mid-life crisis. I have had two more since. In Japan, Duncan Leonard and I had finished the workshop early and agreed over a beer that we just had time to go and climb mount Fuji before we left. All through our two days in that conference room we could see the snow-capped Fuji glistening in the distance. We were both up for it and we started the detailed planning over the next few beers. We had been tempted by the prospect of going up the mountain ever since we had got there, so we just had to go for it, didn't we?

As time passed in the hotel bar we suddenly found ourselves talking more and more about why it may not be such a great idea – we only had work shoes, and it was tight in terms of time. The weather looked like it was closing in and we had no waterproofs. We ummed and aahed for an hour. Neither of us wanted to be the one who stood up and grabbed the other by the collar – let's go! For some reason neither of us could really understand, we then gradually chickened out of making the effort and just doing it. There wasn't really time, we hadn't got the gear … As the final stage in our sad decline we sank down in our chairs and bemoaned the fact that we must both be getting old and pathetic to not take the challenge. It was probably the first time in my life that I had ever really behaved like a grown up, been sensible and mature, at least in a "boys will be boys" area. So we drowned our sorrows to mark the end of an era, had a long snooze in our rooms and just made the flight. I can now track my personal drift from "young and lively" to "older and sensible" to that pivotal moment.

To summarize a few thoughts which you might keep in mind as you get your elephant to dance:

- Key decision makers and resource holders need to be continually involved in the development and implementation process. Successes should be celebrated disproportionately and failures rapidly learned from. Turn the key people and opinion formers who influence the wider community into champions. Ply them with alcohol and die in a ditch to win them over. In support you must promote the IT guys with ambition and charisma to help the new ways of working to really work – no one warms to the agenda of a cold fish, however worthy it may be. Too many specialists who get promoted can be the boring introspective ones, who get off on programming languages, or who enjoy the power they get from controlling the means of production. As the Internet and communications technologies infect and start to underpin a whole lot of bodily functions in your multi-channel organization, the IT guys can become your paramedics on some dangerous days and the first lieutenant you pick to go with you on an expedition on other days. In too many businesses the IT heads can be guardians of the plod and are viewed as the ghastly quartermaster you have to be nice to, to get your battalion's rations.
- A quote which FitzGerald used sometimes at Unilever was:

"The reasonable man seeks to understand the world and adapt himself to it. The unreasonable man seeks to understand himself and change the world to his needs ... All progress depends on the unreasonable man."

I have found this axiom applies beautifully to the new area of Internet innovation and the stretching of the brands in the new economy. I have seen it translated into seismic shifts when my old friend Mike Johnson followed it and when people like Michael Dell, Nelson Mandela and Jack Welsh use variants of it. Everything needs a certain quality of preparation, planning and follow-through, but bloody-minded determination and focus will often be essential to force scale efficiencies and secure high rewards from organizational innovation.

- You need to build an aggressive and balanced approach to driving innovation, so that you learn to succeed or fail quickly and use smart team approaches to network your people together. You also need to make some tough decisions on what you will invest in.

> *Anyone who talks a great game on acetate, but never spills any blood, should be taken out and made to organize events in the community for retired estate agents and lawyers.*

- If you want the revolution to happen you have to secure the radio station and tell your people how to survive the m-bomb.

To address this last point you will typically need a well-orchestrated communication plan to bring the whole organization with you.

The communication and change management process which you devise must aim to:

- generate a sense of excitement about the strategy, and the vision it paints of the future;
- manage the risk that it is portrayed as a headcount reduction exercise;
- engage staff in making the revolution happen, and to counteract the inevitable distractions and sadness caused by reconfiguration of staff numbers and roles;
- create the culture required to transform the scale and nature of the business;
- ensure understanding of the new priorities, at all levels (and those initiatives which are now less important – of which there will be many); and
- develop a sense of common purpose, action and excitement.

Different cultures will need different approaches, ranging from roadshows or conferences through to more participative workshop processes.

If in doubt, do remember that the majority of serious businesses who manage transitions of this type spend as much on training and communication as on infrastructure. It has taken me completely by surprise in my consultancy business how 25% of our support activities in large businesses are focused on this type of education and communication.

The message is: be surgical about slimming the business down and refocusing the people. Then be expansive about engaging the global staff at all levels in understanding and then implementing the change process. An elephant will never dance if the main parts of the body aren't able to pick up the signals from the brain.

The bits that went wrong

Most of the developments and choices in the Unilever story had a happy ending, except perhaps one of the decisions to standardize IT components worldwide. This involved selecting WordPerfect as the word-processing standard worldwide. This was one of many areas where we thought "Mars or Procter & Gamble were not going to be trembling in their boots because we were exploiting the subtle diversity of ten different word-processing packages across the group." It was not a competitive differentiator. It just had to be one common solution to support low-cost purchasing and ease of communication. We didn't choose Microsoft Word, because we thought Bill Gates was a menace and would move us away from our open standards. In most other areas of no-brainer standardization we picked products that stood the test of time and worked well. In this particular area, however, we reacted badly to the supplier.

An arrogant young lad from Microsoft said to us "Isn't 30 million copies of a dominant product an effective standard?" "Ha!" What a stupid view of the world. We even toyed with adopting Unix rather than Windows on the desktop, to force a global scaling and deployment of all systems and applications. We didn't though, thank goodness.

I think that we got the Gates thing a bit wrong. He has done better than I expected.

I have since decided that I can cope with a few extra years of Gates's success with more powerful tools, free browsers for all and the ultimate plug-and-play operating platforms for consumers, which reach directly into businesses internal supply chains and innovation processes. Everyone has the same technology targets to aim at because of the success of the Internet and this man's dominance, and so more of the planet's resources are lining up their invention according to similar end-user principles and technologies. The problem lies, of course, in the level of control and the piece of the action that one company could get on every packet of information that moves between any two people. What is now relatively benign can easily turn into an insidious set of constraints on personal communication and electronic commerce, including a dilution of market forces on the costs of Web access devices (including PCs and their basic software, but also down to portable devices over time). There is now a fairly robust network of people who can see some fairly horrific scenarios being quietly knitted together, stitch by innocent stitch. More of this another day. A fork in the road. A set of choices which are not what they seem. I will discuss another time how some new trampolines are forming which will probably bounce us around the biggest dangers that are lurking here.

For the moment I would be content to let it roll. The key, as we have discussed, is to use these common communication solutions and new ways of working to accelerate everything we do and to network our skills and knowledge. If every village had a different language and currency all those centuries ago we would never have developed a market economy and established trading routes which brought magical spices from the East.

Part 4

The Field Guide and a View of the Future

You are probably now as tired as I am. We have tried to put "life, the universe and everything" for business in the next five years into one book. I believe and hope that in this next five years the stumbling giants will inherit the earth with their great brands – through the efforts of some of their most agile managers and staff. The end consumer will demand value, trust and convenience. A strong brand which comes with efficient and bundled services "However you like today, madam" is my idea of nirvana. It is the blend of traditional service and values and modern performance, accessibility and personalization that gives me a tingle in the spine. How can you fail to be excited?

So let's reflect on the steps required to survive and prosper in the multi-channel world. Let's also look at some of the other forces in the markets which are heading our way (if you are bored by the prospect of a recap go straight to page 178).

Chapter 9

The Big Agenda, the New Surprises and a Trip to Casablanca

Now that the initial froth has gone from the Internet offers and a bit of reality is dawning, we can see the priority actions that every serious business must start to take in the next year or so. To cut to the chase I will draw out a few headlines from the previous chapters.

Checklist of actions

1 Select the broad strategic path that you want to follow – your balance of effort and ambition. If you are a duck you must choose the strategy of a flexible multi-channel duck or at most aim to become a free-flying swan. You should not forget your current brand and travel too far beyond your basic capabilities, but you must extend the proposition so that you can offer the customer a broader offer (Chapter 5).

2 Don't reinvent anything unless you have to – borrow shamelessly from the experience of others and the skills of partners. The thousands of business-years of recent e-commerce experience will get you to the Promised Land, if you can learn from the success and failure of others. This is a new era of transparency in business innovation (Chapter 6).

3 Design your operations to plug and play efficiently – internally and with partners. Build your customer operating model and serve the

hell out of your most important target customers (Chapter 4). Don't treat all customers the same way or they will hate you for it and desert you.

4   Choose your quick wins and your radical options, which give early cost-savings and market impact. Avoid romantic crusades which cannot be translated into hard benefits. Build credibility for your new strategy and organization quickly (Chapter 7).

5   Select the content and infrastructure partners who suit your strategy and quick wins agenda. You cannot make this journey on your own! You need performance-enhancing partners. Choose the right partners in the emerging value chain or you will experience false dawns and hugely expensive flights of fancy (Chapter 5).

6   Develop your transition plan – to help focus priorities and agree major milestones. The normal rules of business planning and the need to make money still apply! (Chapter 7.)

7   Decide how to fund, resource and propel each initiative – be prepared to be bold and radical. This may mean giving equity away and joining a three-legged race with the business equivalent of Carl Lewis (Chapter 5).

8   Kick organizational obstacles out of the way. Educate, simplify and occasionally redeploy the brain-dead to competitors. Spare no expense in realigning people. Take no prisoners in eliminating your permafrost layer (Chapter 8).

9   Succeed or fail quickly. Resource aggressively or starve brutally. Avoid the walking dead. If it can't be delivered in nine months then change the objective (Chapter 8).

10 Enjoy the experience of being part of a massive watershed for consumers, supply-chains and service innovation. The underlying multi-channel bubble which many businesses haven't spotted yet won't burst – so embrace it – avoid the froth at the edges – seize the day.

These ten composite actions are the stuff of life for any traditional success story who want to be around in five years time as an independent business. Interestingly the same challenges apply just as much to new dotcoms or large company spinoffs who are accelerating away from the mother business.

The new economy bust and boom curve

We should briefly go back to the context of what is happening in the markets, before we come to the next wave of mini-bombs which you also need to factor in – once you have started to sort the m-bomb out. To keep your eyes focused on the horizon you need to look beyond the emotional ups and downs in the new economy which could divert or distract you.

I sometimes use the new economy "boom, bust, boom" curve (Fig. 9.1) to illustrate how the multi-channel propositions will roll out over the next two or three years. You can see how Internet euphoria peaked predictably in 1999 and how the inevitable disillusionment followed during 2000. In some sectors we are now into "cross species breeding" and "battle for first brand standing."

The curve gives you a shorthand for how the last few and next few years play out. You may find it useful with colleagues, who mistakenly think that the new economy "trough of despair" (the lowest point) is here to stay.

Atlas Venture are one of the premier venture capital players who have been funding traditional start-ups and a number of the more grounded new-economy plays for many years.

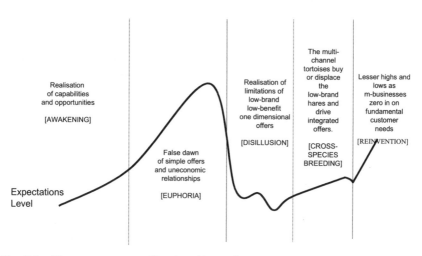

Fig. 9.1   The new economy "bust and boom" curve.

Vic Morris is one of their leading partners. He lives up where the air is thinnest and they climb sometimes without the aid of oxygen and ropes. Vic sums up the post-modernist view of where the smart money is heading:

"We are always excited when we see big established brands building innovative new services off the back of their traditional business. We love nothing better than oiling the wheels of a powerful multi-channel initiative – or putting an entrepreneurial team onto the shoulders of a friendly giant."

Check out how the curve is playing out in your sector (see Fig. 9.2). Plot your position.

Reprise of how to be the first multi-channel brand standing

So let's briefly review how these action areas and highs and lows will play out in terms of practical initiatives and challenges. We know that

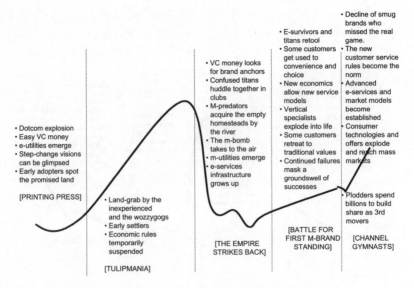

Fig. 9.2   Propositions developing through the new-economy curve.

I managed to avoid buying any technology stocks of any sort during 1999 and most of 2000, as my tax inspector and broker will testify. You could see the Internet bubble growing out of control and the prospect of a false dawn and unrealistic expectations was there in sharp relief. After the inevitable collapse I have recently started drifting into the market for technology companies, who understand how to deliver e-utilities across the channels, as well as the more powerful brands who I believe will be on their multi-channel feet the quickest.

what has happened to customer expectations and traditional retail margins in books, cars and music will inevitably happen in many consumer and B2B markets. The leaders of successful traditional businesses who will prosper are those who will embrace new propositions and the Internet to:

- Get their cost-base in line with (or close to) the best of the start-ups. Most large companies are targeting and achieving cost reductions of 10–15% from existing processes. Some businesses are going for even more radical plans in their smoke-filled rooms. Headcounts are dropping – and they need to.
- Reach the 5 or 10% of existing customers who are looking for greater convenience and richer service with some quick multi-channel solutions – before they are wooed by the enticing new kids on the block. Get your retaliation in first.
- Develop a handful of practical extensions to the current propositions, which will generate new profit streams or will attract some new high-margin customers. In my experience this is easier to do than most people would expect – partly because products and services in most sectors are very inconvenient and often offer very poor value. Remember the speed at which predators are biting juicy great chunks out of the more plodding financial services businesses. Once you build the multi-channel infrastructure to deliver your own products differently you will find many compelling reasons to leverage those capabilities and fixed costs into a select number of adjacent product areas.

- Introduce greater personalization to customers, such as self-service opportunities via the Internet (information, browsing, ordering, account inquiry, what's new/happening), tailored pricing/charging/promotions/range or loyalty schemes which are far more intimate. Personalization is an investment for both the supplier and the customer, but it is a great retention mechanism and it provides a platform to build share-of-wallet.

We have discussed how companies like Walmart, Gap, Chase and Tesco provide excellent examples of how a successful traditional business can raise their game, and introduce these new approaches and business streams without taking their eye off their current profit engines. These businesses are quietly, steadily building greater "share-of-home," as they bring their trusted brand and the convenience of the Internet into the kitchen, the lounge and the study of more and more middle-class and hard-working homes.

Companies like these are a model for brand leaders in any sector.

In addition to the challenge from these born-again brand leaders we have the challenge to traditional businesses from the large company spinoffs, and the more robust startups which combine experience and agility. The most successful examples of this species have recently grown to be nocturnal and live in deepest rainforest. Some of the best business-to-business operations like Foodtrader (an exchange operating in 33 markets) have quietly grown their franchise, and so can appear timid and are rarely seen in the open plains. The more substantial start-ups and spinoffs will emerge gradually into the sunlight and will exhibit outrageous flexibility and multi-channel ambition. This is positively shocking to those of us who have grown up in blue-chips.

This new generation of animals headhunt highly experienced executive teams, who are now often the brightest and boldest thinkers from the blue-chips – enticed by the prospect of equity participation and paper wealth. They know how to partner genuinely with fulfillment companies and non-competing partners – in fact any partner who has skills and resources that they need to get to market fast. Why do they have this openness? Because they have no choice of course – they would grow old and die in Internet time if they behaved in any other way.

The metabolic rate of driving strategy and implementation is very high in multi-channel spinoffs. This ability to move quickly is shared by the predatory brand operations who have forged strong traditional alliances. Their lives now depend on securing first-mover advantage. With low internal headcount and high IT literacy and communication skills the levels of agility and innovative efficiency can be incredibly high.

Such competitors can also make fatal mistakes at staggering speed. But if you believe that every established player will face at least 20 serious multi-channel brand-extenders in the next five years, then you have to assume that at least three will get past your traditional defenses.

The vulnerable company is a classical low P/E *Fortune* 500 business which looks like this:

- They think that partnering is about total quality, vendor specification and forging commercial deals at mutually acceptable margins.
- A large project which takes under a year is viewed as quick and highly impressive.
- At least 50% of the top team may appear to be dead from the neck up, when compared to the wild animals driving startups or the forward-looking tigers like Gall & Gall or Reuters.
- Hundreds or thousands of staff spend countless hours talking to each other, rather than getting out there inventing products, talking to customers, cutting deals with partners and managing end-to-end service.
- It takes six months to raise $2m to pursue a really great innovative idea, if it wasn't in last year's budget. The team which is assembled to drive it is often populated with a liberal peppering of spare parts and lightweights who were temporarily sat on the bench.
- Personal ways of working, innovation processes and communications infrastructure hail from the mid 1990s. E-mail is still viewed as fairly novel. Online teamworking processes are new and the jury is still out on whether they work. Big decisions are still made hierarchically.
- There are so many people and bodies able to interfere in a big play that the machine tends to get stuck. An analogy I like is that the

spectators have wandered onto the pitch, so that the teams can't get on with the game.

If this is you then you might want to panic as follows:

1   Get your spectators off the pitch. Ideally you should chop out the permafrost layer of any complacent senior and middle-managers that you may have (or as a last resort set up a "central services and admin" arm and park all the young and old fogies in there).
2   Adopt best-practice organizational models which support rapid product churn and service innovation (funnels and minimalist structured project processes and all that). Use flat team structures and aggressive sourcing models to underpin it all, with great knowledge management and communication services.
3   Think hard about setting up your own spin-off operations which can attack adjacent or specialist needs areas. Use linked organizations to the mother business which can colonize the future. Stuff them with the guys who are probably about to leave to join the start-ups and have ideas which pass your shareholder value tests. Offer them equity (God forbid!). Give them access to funds and raise further cash via the market if you have to. Companies like Merrill Lynch, General Electric and Proctor & Gamble appear to understand some of these options well, and so should you.
4   Brand the new way of thinking and inventing and create a program to educate all of your people with roadshows. There are many good partners who can help you with this – pack it with your agenda, the wake-up calls from your market and a call to arms. Get all of your people on the edge of their seats and seeing K2 or even Everest in the distance. There is nothing more impressive than a resourceful giant roused from its slumber. Lift the eyes of your people and show them the new horizon.
5   Leverage your cost-base – an efficient branded service provider in the UK or Canada has a raft of relatively fixed costs going into building local marketing communication, product development and added-value infrastructure (e.g. information systems). If you build a set of direct operations in a new territory you can increase the reach of your current business and generate huge amounts of

new value, without major increases in direct costs or physical assets.

Many businesses are learning that these skill levels and costs do not go up significantly when they are targeting 250m consumers, rather than the 50m in their home market. Premium players in sectors which are less sensitive to local tastes are finding that the needs of upmarket customers in Milan are not so different to those in Stockholm – and the growth of regional television and Internet channels is accelerating that convergence. Having achieved some early success and cost efficiencies, they then realize that they have a bigger war chest to fund better communication, R&D and strategic partnerships than the local guy. It is a repeat of the story of Nestlé, Kraft, Unilever and Mars from the 1960s and 1970s, which was fostered by mass-branding and early TV advertising. It is now writ large for the international consumer segments and the multi-channel world.

6   Find partners to build direct low-cost channels. When you thought about entering Benelux or South East Asia you used to decide where you would put your head office, your manufacturing plants, your bricks-and-mortar retail operations. In today's era of direct and online services you will now decide what balance of buying and servicing will be via multilingual call-centers and the Internet, and which local or regional fulfillment businesses can be partnered with to ship the goods, execute billing/payments, handle returns or mail, etc.

The barrier to entry has collapsed in many markets – due in part to the emergence of high-quality execution partners such as Circle/Brann, Tanning, Fedex, Descartes, Unipower, Hewlett-Packard, BT, m-box and a range of other specialists in the key fulfillment areas. Many businesses have found that if you have the right business model and a post-modernist approach to partnering you can enter these new markets within six to nine months, at remarkably low cost and risk.

If you cannot compete on the same footing the marauding masterbrands will outspend you and potentially outsmart you. The only defense in many sectors is to extend your reach and scale, through expansion of the offer and shrewd partnering.

7   A sense of gentle panic is needed – if most of your people really feel that your current approaches are broadly OK for the new marketplace then you will get nowhere until you open their eyes. To address this, try introducing a stretch performance target to help to focus the mind (e.g. generate $5bn of business from new channels in three years). Such targets help to force senior managers to avoid incremental thinking.

You must remember not to give a bright young thing the job to experiment on your behalf. These new channels need hard experience, just like any other line of business. Your experienced people do need to be Internet aware, open-minded and quick witted though. As you confirm your strategy and the business plan for multi-channel initiatives you must include a wider view of value generation in the business case. This doesn't mean that you must use the alternative channels for discounting (which is a crass approach). It does mean using a new and more mature economic model. You must be "intelligently bold."

Ensure that your business is not one of the 80% which will be structurally and culturally incapable of moving fast enough. The economic fundamentals and customer needs are changing so fast that the next two years will probably tell us who has evolved sufficiently to be a serious player in five years time.

You must raise your eyes for long enough to see the m-bomb descending – reaching for the hearts of the lame, the muddled and those of no fixed abode. How prepared are you for this challenge?

A few footnotes for international businesses

Some clear tactics have also come through for the bigger players who are already operating in two or three continents:

• Your platforms for brand management and service packaging of lead products and services must be regional or global. This is usually harder for traditional businesses, who have already established autonomous international operations. Be ruthless about making this happen – it requires an element of charm and robust persuasion with individual operating units.

- Your execution partners, ad agencies and the variety of fulfillment partners should increasingly be selected on a global basis. Common sense will of course prevail, but if you want to be able to compete with global competitors, who can roll successful innovation, consumer communication and procurement deals out at breathtaking speed, then you need to gear up your value chain to do this.

- There will also be increasing pressures to harmonize pricing, ingredients, product specifications and customer management operations internationally. You will need a flexible and powerful set of teamworking and communications infrastructures to underpin this. This does not mean that your operations and local pricing models need to be transformed overnight – but you will need to mobilize your most important ideas, people and partnerships using the smartest processes and infrastructures available. This is very well trod ground in the best businesses such as Unilever, GE and Ford/GM. Find out what they have done and what partners they used and adopt a similar approach – translated intelligently and more efficiently to your market.

- Think hard about how you will signpost your services in the new media world that is now emerging. The dotcoms were flooding traditional TV channels and new channels with waves of advertising. You must plan how you will retain share-of-voice and forge your own partnerships. In the next three years the cacophony of noise in the markets will put severe pressure on your regional communication strategies and your ability to spot the portals and channel partners who will make it.

- Markets like Japan are just as ripe for innovation as Germany or the US. Local consumers in Japan are very used to having luggage delivered to their home when they land at airports, rather than drag it home themselves. Most local shops will routinely deliver almost any small purchase back to your home. This is a market where the power of multi-channel services and the Internet will find a ready home and a great cultural fit.

Adding the customer intimacy challenge

It is now time to turn the hype around one-to-one marketing into a real service and convenience offer across the channels, which feels special and appropriate. We have talked a lot about the challenge for businesses to create a set of basic operational capabilities which operate seamlessly across their traditional retail and the new online channels, in order to:

- Touch different customers in different ways, depending upon their personal interests, needs and requirements. Use thumbnails (m-maps) to mass customize the relationship services and learn as you go.
- Offer lower-cost self-servicing options to customers who want it via their chosen channel – reducing your admin and sales costs along the way.
- Increase sales with the most valued customers, by making the right proactive offers of products that they probably need (based upon what you know about them). These intimate sales offers should be able to be delivered via the full range of traditional and new channels.
- Help the business to understand the needs of customers, transactionally and emotionally, so that new services and product innovations have much more chance of hitting the spot. Speed and iteration (the P.R.I.C.E Approach) will be key to achieving that goal.

The words are easy and fluffy and the benefits are obvious – so what do the lead players do to make this happen on the ground?

The hard experience that we have unearthed together suggests that there are a handful of changes that you need to make in how you do things (and a few infrastructures you need).

1   All the staff who deal with customers need to know a few key things about each customer they face, which can help them to treat them appropriately. This can be at the checkout, on the phone, at the

office or on the doorstep. When staff see the status, likely needs, contact history or risk profile of the customer, they should have been trained to use the information to treat them in the appropriate manner. In all cases an informed "customer welcome" process must precede the specific transactional activity that the customer has come in for. If you miss this, you miss the opportunity to build the relationship and offer them something new.

2   Most companies have general marketing functions, but they don't have customer segment managers who ensure that their "mass-customized" segments have the right proposition, at the right price, through the right channel. Someone has to be fighting to ensure that the upmarket loyals are given a tailored set of offers which meet their needs – and that their contribution meets the increased target of 17% or $200m this year. If your operational design is right, then these segmented offers need not cost you more money to deliver. Go visit the leading banks and the best food retailers who are building their new service models. See how they are engineering their businesses to operate this way efficiently.

3   The voice of the customer needs to be heard down through to the heart of research and development. As people move to the mass-customized approaches, more companies are looking at using antennae customers in the major segments as partners in the innovation process. These are the customers whose thinking and needs are a little ahead of the pack. The Internet and the new multimedia technologies available through to the workplace (B2B) and to the home (B2C) make it possible to use one-on-one online dialogs to:

- Test new creative and communication approaches with sample customers, without the cost and time delay involved with traditional "research" methods. The testing process is really presented as pre-launch dialog to valued customers – with the early response providing the opportunity to iterate content, focus and offers.

- New services and products can be tested by customers at a very early stage. Views, requirements and issues are captured via Web-based knowledge systems. Antennae customers see this as a reward for loyalty. The most valued and innovative accounts are helping you to invent the future (and succeed or fail quickly). The customer becomes part of the late-stage R&D team – which can then move rapidly into full development and launch.

4   An operational customer "hub" is the essential infrastructure needed to store and switch the pivotal customer relationship data between customer access points and back into different product and service divisions. The hub ensures that customers can always feel recognized in a coherent and highly personalized way, from the Internet to face-to-face channels. It is the beating heart of the relationship service for any customer-centric business. The great news is that a high impact set of hub services can now be implemented within six to twelve months, and at a fraction of the cost of doing so five years ago – largely because the technologies and delivery applications are so mature now. There are two or three serious choices to be made, and then as much business design and staff training/reorganization is needed as IT investment. If you get it right fairly quickly the infrastructure will pay for itself one hundred times over – and what a prize if you can do it.

The mini-bombs

We should now turn to the mini-bombs and aftershocks which will keep us company, as the effects and opportunities of the m-bomb play out. I cannot see any of these forces of darkness and light changing the main agenda. Under any scenario you must learn to integrate the evolving set of customer channels and broaden the offer with a range of well-chosen partners.

The mini-bombs will however add a fair amount of color to the journey over the next five years, and will create the odd pothole which will slow progress and cause the heart to miss a beat now and then.

I have tried to focus the following issues and trends on the practical side of life. There will be no shortage of other innovative froth, breakthrough technologies and highly stimulating sideshows, which will carry new buzzwords and dramas into our newspapers and into our lives.

A continuing stream of new access devices

We have talked about a number of mobile and home technologies which sort of work for some consumers, but which are still evolving. The new range of palm devices such as the handspring and the new Bluetooth hand-helds from Hewlett-Packard are a good option today for the computer literate consumers and sales people. It is obvious though that the mobile phone, as we see it today, is a really pathetic online access device. Your nephew may use it for simple SMS messages

The most exciting innovation for consumers and the Internet in the next three years is going to be the successors to the new mobile tablets, which people like Fujitsu are making. These mobile RF devices have large touch-screens like a PC and stay in contact with the Internet via the remote cradle, which sits by the phone socket or the cable box.

At last you don't have to creep upstairs furtively to your den to book a holiday or buy the groceries. You don't get lonely any more. National Semiconductor and others are driving supply up and prices down. I can sit in the lounge or the kitchen next to my daughter and we can mess around on the tablet, looking at dive sites or checking out twintip skis. The power and the touch of the PC with the mobility of the phone for $600. Those backing the two-way nature of digital TV to sell clothes and perfume had better look at how much better the mobile tablet and your Website (linked to the TV advert) will work than the silly little zapper and the back-channel on the TV. You can still offer services on the TV, but use these more intuitive devices for the consumer response. Another multi-channel option. Another eagle has landed. The successors of the mobile RF tablet will contribute strongly to the growth of new marketing approaches and consumer purchase behavior than we have seen up to now with the PC – bolted to the floor in the coldest part of the house.

and it is great for some business uses such as "call the office for new call schedule" for a sales guy. Or perhaps "we have a delivery problem – hit 1 to confirm the same slot tomorrow" for a consumer. There are however only 26 consumers in any developed country who could possibly be motivated to enter a complex grocery order or book a hair appointment and confirm the styling details using a mobile phone. Normal people won't take five to twenty minutes to key in such things using a phone keypad. Similarly the PC is not a ubiquitous and intuitive device for many households. For the next few years, the high street, the normal phone and the office or home PC, will mix and match for most of us. The mobile cavalry will come along gradually to switch more people onto online channels.

Motorola's deal with Symbol in the US is putting barcode scanners onto millions of mobile phones. Barcodes can be put into lots of business places or kitchens in homes to scan a recipe, scan a delivery slot, charge other shopping services automatically via your normal phone bill. Don't underestimate the power of the barcode to codify almost any simple transaction.

Over the next few years you will see a lot of shortcuts like this putting "scancodes" on digital TVs, in catalogs, in magazines, on coupons, on direct mail and around town. Scancodes or later innovations will be used for all sorts of deals for me, shortcuts to register and order, plus other codified complex transactions for all types of B2C and B2B interactions. They will combine intuitively with a new generation of friendly one-touch mobile devices. The innovation of these devices and the price point will continue to surprise you. Markets like Mexico have now got mobile Internet portals (such as Wau) which will bring online penetration to countries with under-developed traditional communications services. Watch these services go ballistic when 3G mobile technology comes in (200 times the current transfer speeds to your mobile phone).

I am entranced by what Sony and NTT DoComo are up to in Japan, as they collaborate with their respective PlayStations and i-mode cell phones. The simple agenda is one of games across mobiles and consoles, but the model for wider business propositions is clear.

In our customer operating model and multi-channel businesses these are just another set of channels and relationship processes. If you have structured your business and your "multi-channel middleware" well, your people should be able to drop in each new access technology and transaction model within a few months at most. Easy as 1-2-3. *Plus ça change – plus c'est la même chose.*

The growth of cross-channel utilities and agents

E-services specialists will slowly mature and will make outsourcing of non-differentiating (but very powerful) utilities much more easy for businesses. Finance, HR, supply chain and many back-office functions managed by specialists will plug and play with internal brand and customer management activities. One can also easily foresee a growing set of automated agents, who act on the consumers' behalf to filter mail and select personal services according to programmed requirements. Anyone who currently has to cope with the nightmare of information, half-intelligent search engines and disingenuous brokers who infest the Internet knows that the personal broker, filter and navigator is long overdue. Really usable technology will take a while to drift in – but the consumer need is becoming strong enough to fire the innovation that will deliver these tools. This is not about AskJeeves – but the far more subtle and personal tools that are now in the labs.

I think that this aspect of "chapter two" of the Internet, as Hewlett-Packard call it, will really cut most ice further up the supply-chain than these customer-facing operations. Every masterbrand who deals with the customer (Walmart, Tesco, Coke, Nike, Sony, Ford) will extend the offer using the more complex partnerships we talked about. Every product can be offered bundled with a warranty, via a dynamically selected insurance partner. Every service may need installation and often delivery. Every vacation, pension or microwave will need another product partner.

Across all these partnerships we will need common e-services applications and processes, which provide the "plug and play" backbones for these sophisticated supply-chains. Utilities and "applications on tap" will be used by the business partners to set up products, activate them, identify customers, process payments, provide white-label facilities for the administration of the service or policy, execute the fulfillment request, tally the nett service rebate and pass customer data on a need-to-know basis. You will see lots of specialists and lots of specialist multi-channel services which oil the wheels of more flexible propositions.

Integrated support applications like Baan (already appears to be dying) and SAP (soon to hit the wall) will be slowly replaced by these far more flexible agents, utilities and one-touch applications. They will navigate the channels and business intersections to perform tasks efficiently between businesses.

The security and "invasion of space" thing

I hate to mention this one, because the thought police tend to use fears of payment security as reasons why consumers and business partners won't use online channels.

The truth is that ergonomics and horrendous customer experiences are much more of a limiter to the uptake of new channels than worries about security. Credit cards are generally safer on the Internet than in the hands of your local waiter – and a reasonable percentage of consumers know that.

The problem is that the bad guys and the online traffic-hijackers who crave online footfall will not be able to resist corrupting the way that the Internet works. With the Internet it is strangely OK for shopkeepers or strip-club owners to grab people on the online sidewalk and bundle them into their premises – and even to lock them in and force them to look and listen (well almost – you can always switch the PC off or close your eyes). This pothole exists for both the direct Internet users and the processes which use the Web behind the scenes. The Web is so anarchic in many ways that it is very hard to defend against these practices and the many more subtle ones which are coming along.

In the porn world they have long been hijacking traffic from legitimate sites and grabbing the consumer dialog. In a much publicized case recently the online computer games site of New World was intercepted via a clever approach called "mousetrapping" – so that innocent browsers got diverted to a maze of porn sites, which they can't escape from. The back button gets disabled and navigation is hijacked – you only get to escape by shutting down. Soon you may have to move electronic house to escape. You can imagine how tedious and offensive it is to be locked into a sex site in Australia when you clicked on a local gardening site, with the intention of buying a lawnmower.

Without boring you with the details, this can happen when Websites get copied and replicated illegally. Up to 3% of the Web is currently being corrupted in this way, my inside sources tell me. Hijacking traffic for porn sites makes them intrinsically more valuable (online traffic or footfall = value), but for other sites the random purchase decision and benefits from grabbing passing trade will encourage similar nasty habits.

We will see a hundred scams and scares of this sort in the next two to three years. The recent fuel blockades and protests caused by the high oil price brought Europe to a near standstill in the summer and fall of 2000. Similar efforts will also happen in the Internet and the multi-channel world – as we start to depend completely on these e-services and tools. Flooding the Web with spurious traffic will create more disruption for protestors than marching in Time Square. We have no long-term experience of how to protect and police these services, so there are bound to be dramas.

In my view they will seem cataclysmic when they happen – but they will all be mastered and they will pass. You should expect these security and confidence potholes and steer around them. Build the defenses into your operating model. Don't panic. Use checks and balance in the physical world to act as a safety net in the online world. Use private intranets to manage the life-threatening processes.

Competition between the channels is doomed to fail

I keep seeing companies trying to do things online which will only ever work in traditional channels. People may buy the second golf sweater in a different color on the Web, but the wedding dress is always going to be a high street thing. The guys like J C Penney and Lands End who are spending a relative fortune on online mannequins will never tell you if your rear end will really look big in it. I am always astonished when companies go into denial on the need for the different channels to do different jobs, and complement each other. Who will ever trust a computer image to help them select a new fragrance, for example?

We will continue to see people investing in new online services that consumers will never use. Horses for courses will develop and new purchase behaviors will evolve – but only sad people will ever divorce themselves completely from the physical world. Embrace a range of complementary channels and you will avoid spraying money up against the wall, building online images of your body or the ridiculous virtual reality stores which parrot a physical store. Each channel should do the job that it does best.

I love it when I see Garden.com or Lucy.com deciding finally to put out paper catalogs. Companies like Lands End have known for years how the offline and online channels complement and reinforce each other.

The three legged race will be seen to thrive

The Toys "R" Us initiative with Amazon may not have met all its objectives, but the collision of old brand with the new metabolism is a great one. In Europe the traditional home-shopping retailer Great Universal Stores bought the new-economy start-up Jungle at a snip. Jungle had all the infrastructures and metabolism to make online electrical and games retailing work – so the marriage of old and new makes me finally want to buy the shares. Tesco use deals with Otto Versand and Grattan to underpin their non-grocery product ranges and services. Reuters use worldpop to diversify the tone and appeal of their offer to younger segments. When I see FedEx getting into bed with the US postal service I wonder where that three-legged team will end up. Think about FedEx drop-off boxes in the 38,000 retail postal outlets around the country (remember the m-box example).

Don't be surprised when you see who buys up the pure-play dotcoms at bargain prices as they hunt for safe harbors. Many will acquire a live wire, because they will find that the mother business is too slow and moribund to reinvent itself. Don't be surprised also when Microsoft, AOL, Yahoo!, Oracle, Cisco and a raft of other technology businesses start to acquire retail and service businesses, so that they become multi-channel end-to-end operational service businesses. I find some of these trends hard to read in any detail – but you can see formidable and threatening competitive forces coming out of these innocent plumbing companies. Those that can do total lifestyle and market infrastructures, as well as the more obvious services, will capture very high levels of share-of-home and business transaction fees. With Oracle reportedly looking at 30 service business prospects every week and Cisco acquiring 20 plus each year, these guys will soon have acquired complete "wall to wall" service and utility businesses. These total business infrastructure propositions should both excite and frighten you.

Propositions will still need to be tailored to local needs

Please don't forget that a number of local tastes, habits and regulatory hurdles will be with us for some time. The simplistic world of the global village that you occasionally read about is still a long way away. Here are a few examples of why you need to get the details right locally, or you deserve to fail at the first fence:

- In Germany it is still illegal to do two-for-one offers (known as bogoffs – buy one get one free). If you tell a German to bogoff he is likely to poke you in the eye and see you in court. Promotions, sales incentives and merchandising arrangements will always demand a little local knowledge and tuning. The devil is in the detail.
- Duties for cross-border business can be one-third of the end price in some countries.
- In France you can't advertise alcohol. It will be fun to see how the government copes with the Web in this area.
- There is no sales tax on books in the UK, or food. This makes life easier for Amazon or Barnes & Noble than it would be for Home Depot.

I could go on – but you can see how powerful the partnering model is. The international brand powerhouse joins forces with the feet-on-the-ground local implementer and proposition extender, who knows all the local rules. You don't get this when you simply recruit a few smart young local MBAs in downtown Milan or Boston.

Multilingual services and speech interfaces will grow in importance

Don't forget that the content on the Internet will be less than 50% in English by 2005. The arrogance of the Anglo-Saxon will then be tempered by hard commercial realities. We have talked about multilingual call-centers, which partners can bring in to complement your core single-language operations. You can also rely upon the IT partners to offer multilingual variants of their products and a range of translation agents, which will gradually provide more options which can extend the reach of strong brands. If the English-American or English speaking players are too slow to see the opportunities and risks in this area, I can see the leaders in continental Europe and the Far East and India finding a competitive edge.

One or two timely reminders

The mini-bombs will cause serious perturbations here and there. We will see a steady stream of new management challenges lapping against the business shoreline. I believe though that for the next three years the challenges of the m-bomb itself will dominate your agenda. You need to get "fit for purpose," to deliver the more rounded customer services and offers very quickly now. Your response to the multi-channel opportunities we have discussed will be make or break for your business – in a way that total quality, the Internet novelties, JIT and the fluffier end of the one-to-one stuff never could.

But let's not forget the evergreen capabilities and skills which are more important than ever in the m-world:

1 *Brand* – many retailers and a surprising number of major manufacturers are pretty sloppy at professional brand management, even in yesterday's world. They will have to get up the learning curve very fast now. Your multi-channel brand management and marketing skills will govern how accurately and surely you can propel your brand into the new relationship and proposition areas. Brand is more important than ever before. A poorly structured and com-

municated brand will get lost in the noise of the new fragmented markets, at a speed that will take your breath away.

A brand that is inconvenient, of questionable value or untrusted will find its position attacked on all sides. Brand predators will eat you alive, whether or not you have joined every procurement club that is out there. Brand is the once and future king.

2   *Product performance* – products that deliver great cleaning performance, best-in-class investment results or wonderful picture quality at an affordable price should continue to thrive. Poor products available at the speed of light will die in a ditch – thank goodness. Please don't mistake the need for customer intimacy, trusted brands, and multi-channel convenience for a lack of priority on product performance.

The reverse is not true however. A truly great product with poor multi-channel presence and distribution will head off inevitably to where the light doesn't shine. So keep your links going with hairy-backed product innovators – but make sure you harness their shining new inventions to a great multi-channel machine.

3   Customer listening – if you have too much arrogance to listen to your target customers, and mould your services to their basic needs, it won't work. Too many businesses still try to cerebrally drive the market towards needs areas which don't really exist. Customer understanding and an intimate knowledge of where customer behavior is heading will be vital in most businesses.

So the usual mix of the old values and disciplines and the new multi-channel approaches will provide the perfect cocktail for success.

The last word

I fleetingly mentioned an old friend, Iain Anderson, who was probably the most innovative of Unilever's directors and is now chairman of BT in Scotland. Iain is always buzzing with ideas and is in demand on business and speaking platforms around the world. Iain and I were chatting over dinner a few months back and he summarized the current situation perfectly:

> *"I have seen enough now to know that this is a once in a lifetime moment – no, a once in 500 years moment. From the last five years to the next ten, we will see changes in the way that we live, trade and collaborate that will dwarf the changes in any similar period in history."*

This has to be the most stimulating time there has ever been to be ducking and diving in the markets or to be a consumer. The multi-channel game that is now on will beat any game show on any channel near you. It may come upon you slowly during the coming months, but these shockwaves will test all of your prejudices about product and service and will send your pulse racing like only sport or sex can.

I shall close with my all-time favorite quote from Casablanca, which summarizes the era of the m-bomb beautifully:

> *"If that plane leaves the ground and you're not on it, you'll regret it. Maybe not today, maybe not tomorrow, but soon – and for the rest of your life."*

Rick in Casablanca

Index